UNEQUAL JUSTICE?

ALSO BY ROBERT PERSKE

SHOW ME NO MERCY: A Compelling Story of Remarkable Courage
  (about a boy with Down syndrome)

DON'T STOP THE MUSIC
  (Two teen sleuths with cerebral palsy upset an auto-theft ring.)

AND ILLUSTRATED BY MARTHA PERSKE

*CIRCLES OF FRIENDS: People with Disabilities and Their Friends Enrich the Lives
  of One Another*

*NEW LIFE IN THE NEIGHBORHOOD: How Persons with Retardation or Other
  Disabilities Can Help Make a Good Community Better*

*HOPE FOR THE FAMILIES: New Directions for Parents of Persons with Retardation
  or Other Disabilities*

UNEQUAL JUSTICE?

What Can Happen When Persons with Retardation or Other Developmental Disabilities Encounter the Criminal Justice System

Robert Perske

ABINGDON PRESS / Nashville

UNEQUAL JUSTICE?
What Can Happen When Persons with Retardation or Other Developmental
Disabilities Encounter the Criminal Justice System

Copyright © 1991 by Robert Perske and Martha Perske

This book is printed on recycled acid-free paper.

Library of Congress Cataloging-in-Publication Data

Perske, Robert,
    Unequal Justice?: what can happen when persons with retardation
or other developmental disabilities encounter the criminal justice
system \ Robert Perske.
        p.   cm.
    Includes bibliographical references and index
    ISBN 0-687-42983-8 (alk. paper)
    1. Criminal Justice, Administration of —United States. 2. Fair
trial—United States. 3. Developmentally disabled —Legal status
laws, etc.—United States. 4. Mentally handicapped—Legal status,
laws, etc.—United States. I. Title.
KF9223.P48   1991
345.73'05—dc20
[347.3055[91-20065

"We All Want Johnny Home" (p. 48) is Copyright © 1990 by Linda Powers. Reprinted by permission of the author, Linda Powers.

Material from *Last Rights* by Joseph Ingle is Copyright © 1990 by Joseph Ingle. Reprinted by permission of the publisher, Abingdon Press.

Cover and p. 10 illustration by Martha Perske.

97 98 99 00 01 02 03 04 — 10 9 8 7 6 5 4 3

MANUFACTURED IN THE UNITED STATES OF AMERICA

FOR MARTHA, MY PAL

CONTENTS

UNEQUAL JUSTICE?

PERSKE

CHAPTER ONE

THE REASON FOR THIS BOOK

I t can happen quickly.

Every now and then, people with mental retardation or other developmental disabilities are arrested for crimes they did or did not commit.

Perhaps we have known of such a person—as a customer or co-worker or student or client or patient or parishioner, or even as our own neighbor. And we may have felt a momentary sadness about the arrest, but we usually assume that an arrested person did commit the crime. After all, most of us want to believe that police officers are righteous officials who don't make mistakes. So we watch at a distance.

But we may fail to see that, after all our friendly or professional contacts with such persons, we know them—their morals, longings, strengths, and eccentricities—better than the police ever will. We may also fail to see that the farther they move from us, and the more the criminal justice system absorbs them, the harder it becomes for them to return to their home communities.

They may live for months and years, locked up in some remote concrete and steel building, patrolled by guards and surrounded by walls topped with razor-sharp wire.

Many such people become the loneliest, most friend-forsaken prisoners the system ever sees.

In some states, they become objects in an odd sort of lottery. Officials filter out a tiny number from the many who could have been chosen, guards move them individually before small groups of officials and witnesses—and they are killed.

And so it goes, as Kurt Vonnegut would say.

A decade ago, however—after the surprise arrest of such a person near one of my former neighborhoods—something within me suddenly refused to ever let it go so easily again. Now one question whirls around in my consciousness every time something like that happens:

> *Did that person receive equal justice?* Whether guilty or innocent, did the system treat that person as other citizens are treated when charged with the same crime?

So I put together this book of observations about persons with disabilities who suddenly were caught in the grip of the law. Please see it as my flashlight, turned on for you and beaming its light into a few dark corners of "the system" where these people have been taken.

As the writer, I possess no legal status. But I do have more than four decades' worth of face-to-face contacts with persons who have disabilities—retardation, autism, epilepsy, cerebral palsy, brain damage, and learning disabilities.* Pains have been taken to keep the book simple and unpretentious, and anyone seeking an all-encompassing legal, sociological, academic, or research-oriented effort will not find it here. Neither will you find any grand plan for reforming the criminal justice system.

The emphasis here is on observation, pure and simple.

---

*As much as some persons dislike the term *mental retardation,* it must be used here because the criminal justice system uses the term so extensively to distinguish it from *mental illness.*

Because the system uses intelligence quotients so extensively (even though many of today's experts question whether a person's true intelligence can be described by a single number on a single linear scale), these IQ numbers will appear in quotation marks whenever they are attributed to a specific person.

As mentioned in previous books, I continue to keep faith with the forward-thinking woman in Salem, Oregon, who said, "We are tired of being seen first as handicapped, or retarded, or developmentally disabled; we want to be seen as *people* first" (Perske, 1978, p. 54). This book also complies with *Guidelines for Reporting and Writing About People with Disabilities* (RTC/IL, 1987): Words like *friends, persons, people, citizens,* and *human beings* appear *before* the words for a disability (i.e., a friend with mental retardation).

CHAPTER TWO

OBSERVATIONS IN A NEIGHBORHOOD

Some years ago, on the Tuesday before Easter, around suppertime, 13-year-old Jonathan Brooks* was beaten to death in a small town in the Midwest. A patrolman found his body the next morning in a wooded strip of land between the junior high school baseball diamond and the town dump. He had been battered about the head with a blunt object.

Since no one had been murdered in that town for more than five years, the tragedy ripped a hole in everyone's complacency and trust. The tragedy at once became the number-one subject for discussion in diners and barbershops and on the streets. People shared their shock and disbelief, what they had heard about the crime, and what they thought God or the police should do to the "animal" (a neighbor's term) when they caught him.

Just before Jonathan's death, he had attended the first junior high baseball game of the season, a few yards from the woods where his body was found. The home-team catcher said he saw him sitting in the bleachers behind home plate.

"Jonathan was making fun of the way I was throwing the ball," the catcher said. "He just kept on kidding me. You know, it was all in fun."

More important, however, the catcher said that Jonathan was sitting with a man, "And you could tell they were having a serious conversation." He described the man as about six feet tall, 175-85 pounds, neat, with red curly hair and freckles. Judging the man to be in his early twenties, the catcher thought he might be a teacher from the visiting team's school. That man sitting with Jonathan Brooks has never come forward, and his identity remains a mystery today.

At 7:30 P.M. on Thursday, two days after the death, a detective went to the home of 20-year-old Sammy Rafter and asked him to come to headquarters to help solve the crime. In spite of his slight build and mental disabilities, Sammy jumped at the chance to go to a police station. Just after midnight, the police charged Sammy with murder.

---

*This chapter uses pseudonyms out of respect for the families involved and the sensitive parole deliberations that will someday take place.

Later, Sammy told his parents how proud he was to have helped the officers solve the case. "He acted as if he had suddenly been made a member of the department," his father said.

Still later at a bond hearing, the chief state's attorney said the evidence against Sammy was "overwhelming." But during the trial, the state based its case only on what Sammy had told the officers that Thursday evening. Sammy had waived all rights to have an attorney present and had felt no need to remain silent. An officer claimed he had typed Sammy's final description of the killing and that Sammy had signed it.

Defense attorneys argued that Sammy—who possesses an inordinate desire to please people who represent power and prestige—had been "led into" what he had said to the officers.

The defense showed that numerous lab routines failed to turn up even one item of physical evidence to connect Sammy with the crime—not a single hair or fiber or footprint or fingerprint or human cell. A parade of clinicians described the many disabilities of this 5'7", 140-pound man with a speech impediment, tousled blond hair, and gangling walk. They explained his short attention span, thinking disorders, fantasies of greatness—his significant impairments in learning and judgment and memory. One expert, describing his impaired central nervous system, claimed that Sammy lacked the strength to deliver the brutal blows the victim received. Most important, however, the defense underscored the young man's unabashed eagerness to please the police—to be accepted by them.

As arguments came to a close, both sides called for "justice." But one excruciating contradiction stood out: A brother, an aunt, and an uncle swore that Sammy had been home, puttering in his room, when the crime was committed. On the other hand, three officers claimed that only the killer could have known what Sammy told them on that fateful Thursday evening.

The jury deliberated for three days—then announced a deadlock, but the judge refused to release the jurors. And two hours later, they did reach a verdict: guilty of second-degree manslaughter.

Rejoicing prosecutors told reporters, "The system works," but the defense lawyers insisted that the state had convicted the wrong man.

Today Sammy lives in a Midwest state penitentiary, where he needs around-the-clock protection from other prisoners.

The parents of the victim were so devastated by the sudden loss of their son, they still haven't gotten over it. Some say they never will.

But words can't describe the deep, unrelenting suffering of Sammy and his family. Now the Rafters keep a low profile and suffer alone. Though they used up their life savings in the legal defense of their son, they remain as unbroken as possible because of their inner strength, a caring religious congregation, and friends who stick by them.

• • • • •

Today, most folks in that Midwest town have forgotten the details of the case. Nobody debates Sammy's innocence or guilt in the town's diners and barber shops anymore. Only broad-brush memories remain: Jonathan Brooks was murdered. The cops arrested Sammy Rafter. He received a trial. The jury found him guilty. The judge passed sentence. The cops must have been right.

Even so, I still give in to repeated urges to take out all my clipped-and-mounted newspaper articles on the case and read them one more time. Then, one more time, I wonder what a person like me—with no legal status—might have done. I even daydream about sitting in a bar when a man with curly red hair and freckles, his tongue loosened by five martinis, suddenly spills his guts about what he did at suppertime on a Tuesday before Easter, some years ago.

CHAPTER THREE

MISUNDERSTOOD RESPONSES

Sammy Rafter may have been guilty, as the jury decided, or he may be innocent and a victim of a terrible misunderstanding. Either way, one can't help wondering: Did that young man's responses at the police station contribute to the fact that he was charged with the crime?

No doubt about it, if a detective abruptly asked you or me to come to headquarters, we would want to be prepared with our best thinking and our best ways of responding. Some of us possess large repertoires of responses for such occasions. Others of us possess fewer responses, but those may be so well-practiced that we would come out all right. Those of us like Sammy own repertoires, too, but our disabilities may affect a few of our responses. And unlike folks who know us, officers might misunderstand what we do and say. One or more of the following factors might influence officers who possess little training in understanding people with mental disabilities. But fortunately, anyone who has lived, worked, or relaxed with people who possess one or more of these responses can explain them:

1. AN INORDINATE DESIRE TO PLEASE AUTHORITY FIGURES

For most of us, zest comes from solving everyday problems. Some persons with mental disabilities, however, may not solve problems too well, so they attempt to gain the friendship of authority figures who appear to be good problem-solvers. That's not a bad way to get along in the world when one thinks about it, but it can be dangerous. According to legal scholar James Ellis and attorney/special education professor Ruth Luckasson, some people possess a "particular susceptibility to perceived authority figures and *will seek the approval of these individuals even when it requires giving an incorrect answer.* Such 'outer-directed' behavior suggests that many people with mental retardation will be particularly vulnerable to suggestion, whether intentional or unintentional, by authority figures or high-status peers" (Ellis & Luckasson, 1985, pp. 431-32).

Records show how 37-year-old David Vasquez tried to please Arlington, Virginia, detectives. On January 4, 1984, they approached Vasquez while he was cleaning tables at a McDonald's restaurant and took him to headquarters. With a tape recorder running, the detectives described to Vasquez the murder of a woman who had been raped and strangled with a cord from a venetian blind.

Vasquez repeated several times that he didn't know anything about the crime, until the detectives told him they had found his fingerprints in the apartment. Too naive to believe that policemen would lie, he broke down and cried for his mother. Then he tried to tell them what they wanted to know. Excerpts from the recording transcript, published in *The Washington Post*:

Shelton: "Did she tell you to tie her hands behind her back?"
Vasquez: "Ah, if she did, I did."
Carrig: "Whatcha use?"
Vasquez: "The ropes?"
Carrig: "No, not the ropes. Whatcha use?"
Vasquez: "Only my belt."
Carrig: "No, not your belt. . . . Remember . . . cutting the venetian blind cords?"
Vasquez: "Ah, it's the same as rope."
Carrig: "Yeah."

Moments later, the detectives asked Vasquez about the actual murder:

Shelton: "Okay, now tell us how it went, David—tell us how you did it."
Vasquez: "She told me to grab the knife, and, and, stab her, that's all."
Carrig (raising his voice): "David, no, David."
Vasquez: "If it did happen, and I did it, and my fingerprints were on it . . ."
Carrig: (slamming his hand on the table and yelling): *You hung her!*
Vasquez: "What?"
Carrig (shouting):   *You hung her!*
Vasquez: "Okay, so I hung her." (Priest, 1989)

As the pressure increased, Vasquez suddenly seemed to go into a trance. With eyes turned glassy, he stared at a spot on the table. In this dreamlike state, his meek, pleading voice became low-pitched and steady as he described how he had killed the woman. That eerie statement persuaded the prosecutor to go for the death penalty. Vasquez' court-appointed defense attorneys, however, talked him into pleading guilty and forgoing a trial, in exchange for a sentence of second-degree murder (40 years) and burglary (15 years).

Later, police connected the crime to the real murderer, and Vasquez received a pardon on January 4, 1989—five years to the day after the detectives had approached him at McDonald's.

2. THE INABILITY TO ABSTRACT FROM CONCRETE THOUGHT

Most of us draw interesting abstractions from a number of concrete terms. For example, the cliche "That's the way the cookie crumbles" serves as an interesting abstract response to a perplexing situation. Some of us with mental disabilities, however, may miss the larger meaning. We will look for the cookie.

Unfortunately, concrete-thinking people may quickly and unabashedly waive their right to be silent and their right to a lawyer. They may fail to understand the abstract meaning of the term *right*. Some may think they are being asked to "wave at the *right*" rather than at the *wrong*. After all, nobody waves at the *wrong* in a police station. Others may think it has to do with *right* versus *left*. And even if some know it means more than that, they still don't catch the abstraction that they are giving up their *constitutional rights as a citizen*. Also, to them, asking for a lawyer may be seen as an admission of weakness, so they tell officers they don't need anyone to defend them. They respond much differently from a Mafia kingpin who demands a lawyer, sits down, and shuts up.

3. WATCHING FOR CLUES FROM INTERROGATORS

People who are so dependent upon others for learning to do things the right way often work diligently at reading their interrogators. They listen for words, look into faces, even copy moods in their tries for "correct" answers. Even when they guess, their responses often carry a ring of truth, convincing policemen they're on the right track. One can find transcripts filled with questions to which yes and no answers had been unwittingly mandated by the way the interrogator posed the questions. Example:

Q: "You did see John before he died, didn't you?"
A: "Yes."
Q: "So you weren't at home?"
A: "No."
Q: "When your family said you were home, they were wrong?"
A: "Yes."

Another variation:

Q: "Were you with John?"
A: "Yes."
Q: "Were you with your family?"
A: "Yes."
Q: "You couldn't have been with both of them? Which is it?"
A: (Silence)
Q: "Were you with your family or were you with John?"
A: "With John."
Q: "Let's run that one by again; were you with John or were you with your family?"
A: "Family."

Some people will affirm the choice that was suggested last.

As for attempts to match the moods of others, one example came from a prison guard in Huntsville, Texas, during a dinner conversation. When he learned of my interest in persons with retardation, he said there was a person with that disability on his cell block. He described how other inmates liked to circle the man in the yard for entertainment. According to a plan, everybody laughed and joked, and the man in the center laughed, too.

"Then suddenly, they stopped and looked as sad as they could," the guard said, "and believe it or not, they could make the guy cry!" I had a hard time finishing my supper.

Speaking at the American Association on Mental Retardation, Attorney Clive Stafford Smith described his defense of Jerome Holloway, "a man with IQ 49" who had confessed to a murder:

Sadly, in order to illustrate Jerome's limitations, I had to ask him some questions myself to show what you could to do him:

"Did you assassinate President Lincoln?"

"Yes," Jerome said.

"Did you assassinate President Kennedy?"

"Yes."

Finally, with my fingers crossed, I asked, "Did you assassinate President Reagan?"

"Yes."

This illustrates one of the sad problems we face. In order to get across the limitations of someone with retardation, you have to humiliate the poor guy. But one must go through this rigmarole to show police officers why it was so easy to get the confession they got. (Smith, 1990)

4. THE LONGING FOR FRIENDS

Although we don't think about it too often, most friend-making tends to be an upward-mobile activity. We choose friends we can look up to—people with attractive personalities, power, skill, or status. The idea of being close to people who are "beneath us" doesn't seem so attractive to some. No doubt about it, such leanings are unfair, but until they change, one can expect people with mental disabilities to work eagerly to make friends.

Defense Attorney David Bruck recalls James Terry Roach after his September 1, 1986, execution in South Carolina: "A kid like Terry grows up always being rejected. His playmates get older, more mature, get quicker, get more impatient, and before long, they are bored with him. . . . People like that . . . become the classic sidekick for any psychopath whose path [they] happen to cross" (Bruck, 1989, p. 82).

The trial record acknowledged that Roach had acted under the domination of another man. Interestingly, that so-called normal codefendant received a life sentence for testifying for the state (Amnesty International, 1987, p. 71).

5. RELATE BEST WITH CHILDREN OR THE ELDERLY

Some persons with retardation hang out more with younger people when they fail to relate well with those their age. The person's larger size but less-sophisticated way of thinking can be attractive to children. I recall spending an afternoon at the seashore with such a friend who was nice looking and in his early twenties. For about an hour, he tried to strike up conversations with men and women his own age. After nothing came of the attempts, he moved into the children's shallow area. For four hours he stayed with the kids and emulated a skilled recreation director. He taught the kids to float and stroke. Later, they lined up as he helped each one do a back flip in the water. By the end of the day, everyone in the shallow area knew his name, and his interactions with the children were considered warm and appropriate.

For the same basic reason, some persons with retardation enhance their self-value by helping the elderly in the community. Jerome Bowden, described later, is a perfect example. If a jury had been made up of folks for whom he had delivered groceries or chopped wood, they would have refused to vote for his execution.

6. BLUFFING GREATER COMPETENCE THAN ONE POSSESSES

Anthropologist Robert Edgerton, in *The Cloak of Competence,* describes how he and his colleagues interviewed and gathered data on 48 persons with retardation ("mean IQ of 64") who moved into the community from a California institution. He found that most of them struggled to cope in the community and would not have made it without support from others. Even so, those people with retardation did everything they could to pass as so-called normal: "They are often surprisingly clever in their techniques of passing, and they are always dogged in their efforts." They struggled to maintain self-esteem by hiding their incompetence (Edgerton, 1967, pp. 217-18).

On March 12, 1980, when articulate, well-mannered Johnny Paul Penry took the stand in his own competency trial, he looked and sounded knowledgeable. When someone asked him a tough question, he looked serious, like one in deep thought, then said, "Would you run that one by again?" Even so, a *Dallas Times Herald* reporter described a different situation when defense attorney John Wright questioned his client:

> In answer to question after question, Penry [demonstrated] that he could not read, write, or count, that he did not know the days of the week or months of the year. Nor could he say how many nickels in a dime. "Who is President?" he was asked. Penry brightened, indicating that here finally was one question he could answer. "Nixon," he said proudly. It was 1980, the last year of Jimmy Carter's presidency. (Ellis & Rice, 1988*a*)

7. AN ALL-TOO-PLEASANT FACADE

"Many people with retardation smile a lot," said Judith Menadue, the defense attorney for Herbert Welcome, now on death row in Angola, Louisiana. "But this is related to retardation, not to a lack of remorse. They are anxious for approval, and have learned that smiling is one way to get that approval. But they don't have the judgment to know when to smile." In Welcome's trial, the prosecutor cited Herbert's smiles as evidence that he lacked remorse (Zehr, 1991).

8. ABHORRENCE FOR THE TERM *MENTAL RETARDATION*

This term wounds some people so deeply, they will do almost anything to disconnect themselves from it. For example, when self-advocates from Connecticut, New Jersey, New York, and Pennsylvania met in Princeton, New Jersey, for the First Interstate Seminar on Self-Advocacy for Persons with Developmental Disabilities, this became their most heated issue. A statement from the report:

> The label that people most resented was *retarded*. It hurt when people used that word. One woman said when she was small and they used that word, she had no way of defending herself. Another woman said she just clammed up and she felt less than other people, and she needed to get back to her friends and the self-advocacy group to renew herself. As a result, the conference called upon state agencies to no longer use that word. (InterServ, 1986)

A year and a half later, the self-advocates again met and railed against being called *mentally retarded*. From the second report:

> We still hate the word *retarded*. At the Princeton meeting, it came up over and over. Being called retarded hurts. As soon as you are labeled retarded, you are treated differently. You get shoved to the back of the line. Others stop talking to you. [One person said,] "Some of you here have never been called retarded. So you really don't know how it feels. Take it from me, it hurts. But if you ever feel my feelings, you'll know what I'm talking about." (InterServ, 1987)

And so they crusade. The battle, however, contains an ironic twist. Not being called *retarded* might enrich their lives in the community. In the criminal justice system, however, if the word is not used, they might be imprisoned or killed.

A retrial of Johnny Paul Penry ended July 17, 1990, in Huntsville, Texas, with a sentence of death. The U. S. Supreme Court ordered the retrial because the first trial judge had failed to instruct the jury to consider mitigating evidence related to Penry's mental retardation. Although now the defense presented massive evidence that Penry was indeed retarded, the prosecution still refused to consider it. It even denied it. Day after day, the jury was bombarded with emotional statements: "He doesn't look retarded." "He doesn't talk like a mentally retarded person." "He's faking retardation."

The jury believed the prosecution. On the other hand, if Penry had taken the stand at this trial and had been asked if he was mentally retarded, he probably would have said, "No" (Perske, 1990).

9. REAL MEMORY GAPS

Numerous people on witness stands seem to possess selective memories. And yet some persons with retardation or similar disabilities have genuine memory gaps. For years, memory impairment served as one of the five basic symptoms of brain damage (APA, 1968, p. 22). Even when persons seem to remember everything, their memory can be impaired. In one study, persons with mental retardation were asked for directions to their homes. Fifty-five percent of them gave directions which, although complete, proved inaccurate in significant ways (Kernan & Sabsay, 1984, p. 39).

10. A QUICKNESS TO TAKE BLAME

"Some persons with retardation will determine or assign guilt even when a situation is the result of an unforeseeable accident," say Ellis and Luckasson. "The inability to distinguish between an incident which is the result of blameworthy behavior and an incident which results from a situation beyond the individual's control can have serious consequences" (1985, pp. 429-30). According to Ellis and Luckasson, some persons have pled guilty for crimes they did not commit because they believed that blame must be assigned to someone. And others eagerly assume blame, thinking it will make their accusers like them.

11. IMPAIRED JUDGMENT

In the retrial of Johnny Penry, death-row inmates testified that they all tended to be "out of place" (ignoring a formal rule) when guards were away from their area. When the guards returned, everyone hurried to get back "in place"—except Penry. Somehow he failed to see the difference.

Penry also showed flawed judgment while confessing to the police. Wanting to sound confident and in control, he used prison jargon—the kind of language others would never use with interrogating officers. When he talked about women, he called them *chicks*. When he supposedly fled, he *boogied*. During the trial, the prosecutor used these words repeatedly, leading the jury to see Penry as cocky and without remorse (Perske, 1990).

One might question Gayland Bradford's judgment when, on February 2, 1990, he appeared with a fresh haircut in a Dallas County, Texas, courtroom. It was a carefully sculpted flattop with shaved sides, the sort of thing one sees quite often in urban areas—with one difference: On each of the stubbly shaved sides, the barber had inscribed the unmistakable outline of a lightning bolt.

"Despite the fact that his life was hanging by a thread," reported Ron Rosenbaum, "that thread consisting of the jury's judgment of whether he might be dangerous in the future, Gayland Bradford had chosen a fashion statement that—whatever its private meaning to him—seemed to announce to the jury, '*I am one dangerous dude*'" (Rosenbaum, 1990, pp. 173-74).

Bradford received a death sentence.

12. AN INABILITY TO UNDERSTAND RIGHTS, COURT PROCEEDINGS, OR THE PUNISHMENT

To be found truly competent to stand trial, a jury must agree that a person (1) understands the court proceedings and (2) can assist the attorney in preparing a defense. These two competencies are built upon a clear understanding of the accused's rights and of what the punishment will be if found guilty.

On March 17, 1989, Barry Lee Fairchild, with the help of a new defense lawyer, told a federal district judge in Little Rock, Arkansas, that he had never understood the meaning of Miranda rights until a fellow death-row inmate, William Frank Parker, explained the statement. After reading Fairchild's case file, Parker had said, "Man, if you hadn't confessed, they wouldn't have nothing on you." Parker said that Fairchild thought the Miranda warning "was some routine speech to make a case. . . . They read him his rights and told him what he was going to say, and that's what he did." New Mexico retardation expert Ruth Luckasson, after a thorough evaluation of Fairchild, found the man too concrete in his thinking to understand his rights without a skilled helper who would take pains and slowly explain them in language he could understand (Ault, 1989).

As for knowing what's going on in the court proceedings, one can discover in later chapters how certain defendants—oblivious to what really went on in the courtroom—sat at the defense table and drew pictures (like John Penry), or spoke out loudly and aimlessly (like Tommy Lee Hines). Even some, after years of trials and appeal hearings, still felt they had been imprisoned because they couldn't read or write (like Limmie Arther). A promise to play good basketball after his execution (like Morris Mason) tells us about the failure to understand the punishment.

13. PROBLEMS WITH RECEPTIVE AND EXPRESSIVE LANGUAGE

Think about how a thought travels from one person to another: The message travels via impulses from the brain to muscles that vibrate the air that flutters an eardrum that generates impulses that travel to the receiver's brain. Then, after the message is processed, a response is created and moves back over the same delicate and intricate system to complete two-way communication. Then think how brain damage, sensory impairments, mental retardation, or emotional blocks can throw monkey wrenches into what was meant to be a relaxed two-way flow of ideas.

I recall going to the Topeka, Kansas, police headquarters several years ago to help a 16-year-old with Down syndrome. Earlier, an officer, seeing the boy on the street and thinking he looked suspicious, walked up to him and said roughly, "What's your name?"

The uniform and the voice tilted the boy's communication system like an overmanipulated pinball machine. Trying to compensate for his lack of response, the boy spread his legs, put his hands on his hips, and stared into the face of the cop. Reading this pose as sassy defiance, the officer handcuffed the young man and took him to the station.

"It would not be unusual for a [person with retardation] to be unresponsive to a police officer or other authority or to be able to provide only garbled or confused responses when questioned," report Ellis and Luckasson. "Even when the person's language and communication abilities appear to be normal, the questioner should give extra attention to determining whether the answers are reliable" (1985, p. 428).

14. SHORT ATTENTION SPAN AND UNCONTROLLED IMPULSES

Although myriad sights and sounds strike our sensing mechanisms, most of us can lock onto selected sounds and tune out the rest. Consequently, at a party, we sometimes become so engrossed in a single conversation that the rest of the room's noises—music, laughter, buzzing of other conversations—can be ignored. It sometimes takes a waiter falling down the stairs with a tray of dishes before we lose our focus.

On the other side of this coin, we feel hundreds of unhealthy urgings within us that we would never think of carrying out. So we focus. We act on a few reasonably healthy impulses and keep the rest in check.

On March 11, 1980, at Johnny Paul Penry's first competency trial in Groveton, Texas, Johnny's older sister described the constant supervision Johnny Paul needed to keep from going out of control. According to her, he lasted only a few days in first grade because he could not sit still and pay attention. One day after he ran out of the room and climbed the flag pole, faculty members called the sister to coax him down. The school transferred Penry to a special class, but he went out of control there, too. At home, when not under supervision, he was locked in his room, sometimes for a whole day (*Texas* v. *Penry,* 1980*a*, pp. 443-44, 455).

On the next day of Penry's first competency trial, clinical psychologist Jerome Brown described Penry's attention span and uncontrolled impulses:

> Dr. Brown: [Penry] has very great difficulty controlling himself. . . . The short attention span, the impulsivity has been documented from an early age in this young man.
> Attorney John Wright: What do you mean by that?
> Dr. Brown: He simply cannot do what he's told to do for very long. The word *impulsive* means that he's prey to his own urges or impulses at the moment. He doesn't have the ability to say, "Wait a minute, I'd better not do this. I better wait or better not do it at all.". . . This means that he can't attend to things for any length of time. He can't focus. (*Texas* v. *Penry,* 1980, pp. 558-59)

Ten years later on July 17, 1990, at Penry's retrial in Huntsville, the prosecutor gave his summation. With great anger, he unleashed detail after detail to demonstrate that Penry was the most vicious man he'd ever met and deserved to die. Most people being so debased would freeze in their chairs and pay close attention. But Penry only sat at the defense table and drew pictures on a piece of paper. He glanced up at the prosecutor a couple of times, then returned to his drawing. As the prosecutor continued speaking and Penry continued drawing, a woman in the audience sneezed. Penry turned and looked at the woman. Later, the door to the courtroom opened to sounds of people talking in the hall. Penry turned around and stared at the door—even while the prosecutor continued his vitriolics (Perske, 1990).

15. AN UNSTEADY GAIT AND STRUGGLING SPEECH

Somehow it is difficult for some people's muscles to cooperate. This is especially true of people who have cerebral palsy. Quite often, they are excellent receivers of sights and sounds. When they try to respond, they know exactly what they want to say and do. But the impulses sent to the muscles appear to have been dispatched by a madman. Arms flail, heads bob, and tremendous thought and energy are exerted in an attempt to control their muscles as they shape words and voice them. Sometimes they drool—a behavior a cartoonist might dramatize for a laugh. Actually, the cartoonist is demonstrating ignorance. He or she has never learned that some drooling is caused by inefficient swallowing muscles.

Some of these gutsy people will take as much as three hours in the morning to wash, dress, eat, and get off to work. One will seldom find an ounce of fat on people with cerebral palsy, because they may exert twenty times more energy in walking, talking, and working than the rest of us.

Yet records show that some ill-trained officers have arrested such people for being under the influence of drugs or alcohol.

16. EXHAUSTION AND SURRENDER OF ALL DEFENSES

If overcoming their disabilities requires such beyond-the-ordinary time and energy in order to function as best they can, think what can happen to these people after they spend all day and all night in a police interrogation room. Tired officers are relieved by fresh ones, but arrestees receive no shift changes.

• • • • •

It's easy to see how law enforcement officers could misread the responses of persons with disabilities. After all, diligent officers and prosecutors must latch on to a few facts and develop a belief about a certain suspect. They must become hard-working, unemotional deducers. They must dig and push for facts to support their belief. Even so, if good officers understood—really *understood* the responses of persons with retardation or similar disabilities—they might take these factors into consideration, especially when no motive or physical evidence can be tied to the defendant.

CHAPTER FOUR

DOLORES NORLEY'S OBSERVATIONS

Think about Raoul Wallenberg, who saved thousands of Hungarian Jews from death by standing face-to-face with their captors. Roll that vision into a slender, five-foot, determined woman with the energy of two persons. Then you will begin to picture Dolores Norley. This Florida mother of a son with retardation, a woman who has been a professor of communications and is now a lawyer and a police trainer, unabashedly walks into police stations, courts, jails, and prisons when people with disabilities need an advocate. Sometimes she tries to involve others. When most decline, she calmly accepts the fact that her forays scare the hell out of others. Then she goes alone.

Since the early 1950s, Norley has taught at police academies; logged many hours in patrol cars (especially in Chicago); voluntarily visited the cells of prisoners with retardation; written training manuals for officers, attorneys, and judges; and helped to develop laws to protect persons with retardation or similar disabilities.

Norley never seems to operate like a wildly aimed howitzer. Instead, she spies a specific injustice, does "homework" on it, and then takes direct aim at the problem. Witness the following points she makes in her speeches and articles:

The Criminal Justice System Is a Confusing Place.

● It doesn't even know what itself is about. It is torn between rehabilitating, punishing, and deterring people. One court can act like John Wayne, another like Mother Teresa—for the same crime. One judge can have the spite of a vigilante, another the wisdom and intellect of Justice Brandeis.

● The system isn't always rational. Tom Wicker, a political columnist for *The New York Times*, held himself responsible for the deaths of many prisoners in the Attica prison uprisings. In *A Time to Die* (1975), he describes how prisoners asked him to represent them in the mediation

24

sessions. He went to the meetings and he blamed himself for assuming that the system was rational. It was not.

● Sentencing practices can be arbitrary, discriminatory, and generally unprincipled. They are often governed by the subjectivity of the judge and influenced by the current vacillating public feeling about any given offense.

● Some members of the system, nevertheless, are educable. More often than not, they are eager to do right, to learn about the people they are dealing with, and to be inventive in their jobs when they have the right guidance and persuasion (Norley, 1984).

Except for those arrested for murder, rape, and child abuse, the system would like to spit out people having retardation. But it doesn't know how. The police, attorneys, and judges have set things they must do—even if the person with retardation doesn't fit the usual criminal mold. That's professionalism (Norley, 1984).

When persons with retardation enter the system, it is not just a crisis, it is a disaster. I know of no intellectually diminished person who has returned from prison an improved person. It ruins them. It teaches . . . how to survive by evil means. Since they are often unable to choose proper behavior from improper, they bring with their release all the street knowledge and methods [of their fellow inmates] which will be unacceptable on the outside. Then you have a perfectly trained recidivist (Norley, 1984).

The First Step: Educating the Police and the Courts

● I do everything I can to organize programs for training the police, lawyers, and judges—even getting them to carry wallet cards that list helpful hints and the local disability agencies on call to them. In my experience, officers who can recognize and delineate disabilities become ambassadors. Once their awareness is raised, they are amazingly helpful in avoiding inappropriate arrests (Norley, 1986).

● Community level judges, if approached, will often welcome conferences with local people on possibilities for special programming (Norley, 1984).

● The police of every country are eager to know the facts on retardation. They don't enjoy having to be unsure, wary, fearful, or hostile in their approach. They see themselves, properly, as the guardians of safety and harmony. They are appalled when faced with the possibility of an inappropriate arrest caused by their having too little understanding of a new situation. You will never have an audience hungrier for information than a police class (Norley, 1972a).

● Police can be taught that they have a wide range of actions available to them when they accost a person who may be retarded and may or may not have committed a crime. If it is clearly a law-breaking, then that is a different matter. Their routine for apprehension and arrest is defined in that case. But more often than I like to remember, people with retardation are arrested because the police officer doesn't know where to turn, and the myths about retardation have him a bit more uptight than he might otherwise be (Norley, 1974).

[Norley developed a curriculum for training police under the joint aegis of The President's Committee on Mental Retardation and The National Association for Retarded Citizens.

This was made mandatory for Florida police training in 1972 and later in Georgia. It is the base of training across the United States, Canada, and parts of England and Ireland, where Norley has conducted training sessions. One of the many national and international organizations included in the development of the PCMR/NARC curriculum product is the International Association of Police

Chiefs. That association has produced a training key—#253: *Contacts with Individuals Who Are Mentally Retarded* (IAPC, 1980). It includes a remarkable "street test" which officers can use upon encountering a suspect or a person in need. It contains 23 simple questions related to physical appearance (e.g., "Can the individual easily button his or her coat?"); speech and language (e.g , "Can the person give coherent directions from one place to another?'; educational level (e.g., "Can the person recognize coins and make change?"); and social maturity (e.g., "Does the person tend to answer yes or no questions affirmatively, even if a yes answer seems inappropriate?"). "Keep in mind," she writes, "that the purpose of street testing is not to affix a prejudicial label to the individual . . . it permits the officer to recognize appropriate *helping* responses."]

Those Who Work with Persons Having Retardation Need Educating, Too.

• An example: A teenager with retardation went to his teacher at school to ask if a recent activity (fondling the genitalia of a young boy) was okay. The teacher sent him to the counselor. The counselor called the police.

The young man was given 30 years in the penitentiary (even though rapists in Florida only average five years). The judge did it because he had suddenly become horrified by the current mushrooming of sex-act cases.

When other prisoners saw the young man as a potential sex object, he requested protective custody. That amounted to being in absolute isolation—no radio, no reading material (he can't read anyway), no exercise, no meals outside his cell. At the time, he was 18 and flabby. When we tried to get him into a sex-offender program, he was refused because "he has less than normal intelligence."

When I visited, the guards put handcuffs on him and two armed guards stood outside his cell door. Handcuffs are rough when you are wiping away tears.

Whether his is a case of true pedophilia or a case of situational sex play, we may never know. Soon he may either go mad with the isolation, or become so desperate he will be willing to go on the compound and accept the protection of a "lover" (Norley, 1984).

The Earlier a Person with Retardation Is Diverted from the System, the Better.

• If the crime is reprehensible such as in capital cases, officers and courts have few options. Otherwise, persons with retardation need to be helped out of the criminal justice system and placed into alternative arrangements as early as possible—first appearances, preliminary hearings and arraignments. Sentencing hearings are important, too. If we can offer alternative programs, many courts will jump at the chance to try them (Norley, 1990).

• While working on a committee investigating Miami's Youth Hall, I had the soul-searing experience of finding dozens of inmates with retardation in a hellish environment. They had merely been picked up for loitering, having seizures, truancy, and other noncrimes, with no hope of release or review for months or years. No lawyers. No advocates. No understanding of rights (Norley, 1972*b*).

No attempt is made to excuse people with retardation from the consequences of their actions. Hear me loud and clear on this point. In a world where we are finally moving people back into the communities—where everybody belongs—it would make no sense to demand a double standard. In a normalized world, one has to live within society's rules. To the extent that those rules are not discriminatory, we must accept them. Beyond that, we should rebel and try to change the rules and laws (Norley, 1984).

• I don't mean to suggest that all people with retardation are therefore not culpable in their criminal acts. But I do believe strongly that for the same act, a person with normal intelligence is more likely to escape being caught and to avoid punishment (Norley, 1985).

More of Us in the Field Must Become Assertive Interveners.

• Judges will change. Prosecutors and public defenders will go on to cushy jobs in big firms. Only the advocates will remain constant. We must get to parole boards with facts about retardation as well (Norley, 1985).

• The biggest hurdle is the diffidence of those who work with people having retardation. It is easy to blame the system for being insensitive. Then we become intimidated by them and don't try to advocate. We think we'll be blocked. Not so. Court liaison work is exactly like any other form of advocacy. The rules are identical: Do your homework. Know the problem better than they do. Know some of the solutions. Realize that some folks inside the system are frustrated, and they will welcome you and your expertise (Norley, 1984).

• Almost always, I work as an intervener with no status. But I am always welcomed. It works because the courts are desperately looking for any help they can get. Recently, I went into a court and introduced myself as a person with no status—except for thirty-three years of experience in the field of retardation. The judge said, "Thank God! Do you have a card? I have a few other cases I want to talk to you about" (Norley, 1986).

Finding a person incompetent to stand trial may not always be a good thing. It could lead to a lifetime of incarceration in an institution and thereby deny him or her a chance to be proven innocent (Norley, 1990). [Norley has joined other Floridians in putting through a bill that speaks to this issue. Florida statutes state that any person found incompetent to stand trial can be incarcerated for only two years. If the defendant remains incompetent after two years, the charges shall be dropped.]

Psychiatrists are dear to the heart of the courts. The courts were long ago intimidated into accepting them as the authority for practically everything. We, as never before, need educators and psychologists who have worked with persons with retardation as our evaluators and expert witnesses. We must plan end runs around psychiatrists (Norley, 1990). [Norley joined others in successfully separating the Florida statutes for mental retardation (Chapter 393) and mental illness (Chapter 394). In guidelines she has written for police and the courts, she believes that psychologists and educators trained in developmental disabilities are the best evaluators and expert witnesses in cases having to do with retardation and similar disabilities.]

But We Need the Alternatives.

The sad fact: Nine out of ten times, it is the lack of alternatives—not the nastiness of the court—which sends our people to miserable incarceration where they are the prime victims of others there. We *must* create alternative programs (Norley, 1990).

CHAPTER FIVE

JEROME BOWDEN'S ELEVENTH HOUR

 athryn Stryker, 55, suffered a brutal death in her Columbus, Georgia, home on October 11, 1976. Her killer beat her with a pellet rifle and, after her death, plunged a butcher knife into her chest. Police discovered the body three days later and arrested her next-door neighbor, James Graves, age 16. The next day, they arrested 24-year-old Jerome Bowden. Stryker was white; Graves and Bowden were African American.

Graves, being a minor, received a life sentence. However, he later was found insane and was sent to the state hospital for the criminally insane, where he remains to this day. Bowden, on the other hand, received a death sentence just 56 days after his arrest. He became the ninth man on death row from Columbus, a city of 17,000—the most from any city in the state.

So fifteen days before Christmas, the criminal justice system began to click down on Bowden like an irreversible ratchet, pausing only for the necessary court appeals as they came up. Then came the final order from the Muscogee County Superior Court that Bowden must die not later than noon on June 24, 1986. His date with death was set for June 17 at 7:00 P.M.

Monday, June 16, 1986. The Georgia Supreme Court and the 11th U. S. Circuit Court of Appeals denied Bowden's last appeal. He was moved to the holding cell a few feet from the electric chair. Prison officials, guards, and execution experts busied themselves on task after task in their ritualistic preparation for the forthcoming execution.

Tuesday, June 17. The five-member Pardons and Appeals Board suddenly stopped the ritual. According to the board, the 1976 trial court failed to consider Bowden's diminished mental capacity. They ordered a 90-day stay of execution to allow evaluators to examine him.

This surprise action infuriated the man who had prosecuted Bowden ten years earlier, according to a report in the next day's *Atlanta Constitution*: "We are upset that a non-judicial body has disregarded the facts of the case."

Board chairman Wayne Snow stated that a team of Emory University psychiatrists on contract with the state would examine Bowden: "I'd like to know what degree of retardation he has and does he know right from wrong."

THE FACTS BEHIND THE SURPRISE STAY

A month before Bowden was scheduled to die, one of Bowden's attorneys had asked Patricia Smith, president of the Association for Retarded Citizens in Georgia, for help. Smith, a social worker and teacher experienced in working with persons having retardation, had recently received a law degree, and though she had no experience as a criminal lawyer, she immediately went to work. What she discovered and what she did stopped the execution in its tracks.

Smith's brief filed with the Board of Pardons and Appeals made three powerful points:

1. *"Jerome Bowden has mental retardation and is intellectually incapable of comprehending the meaning of death."* Smith reinforced this point with a thorough 11-page biography of her client's life.

2. *"The question of Jerome Bowden's competency was never tried."* Smith discovered that her client's court-appointed attorneys raised the question of competency, but when the trial judge suggested they withdraw the motion, the two young attorneys, failing to recognize Bowden's mental retardation, followed the judge's suggestion. Appellate courts also refused to look at Bowden's retardation because the trial court had failed to do so first.

3. *"No evidence linked Jerome Bowden to the crime, and he could not have read or understood the confession drafted for him by police."* In Smith's words:

> Jamie Graves, Jerome Bowden's co-defendant, implicated Mr. Bowden in the crime in a signed statement Graves gave to police before Mr. Bowden was sought or charged.
> Jerome Bowden turned himself in to police as soon as he was told by his sister that the police were looking for him.
> No physical evidence whatsoever was found to link Jerome Bowden to the crime. The only evidence of his participation in the crime was his purported "confession," which was drafted and typed by police and which Mr. Bowden could neither have read nor understood if it had been read to him. By the state's own evidence:
>
> 1. A wig, allegedly used during the crime, was found on a couch in Jamie Graves' house.
> 2. Jewelry, taken during the crime, was found in Graves' house.
> 3. A pellet gun, used in the crime, was found under Graves' house.
> 4. Pawnbroker Sammie Roberts testified that he received a television set, taken during the crime, from Graves and gave him $10 for it. He also testified that he had never seen and did not know of Jerome Bowden.
> 5. The operator of a coin shop stated that he bought some coins, taken during the crime, from Graves.
> 6. No fingerprints of either defendant were found in the house where the crime occurred.
>
> Jerome Bowden testified at his trial that he had told police that he did not participate in the crime.
> Mr. Bowden also testified that he only agreed to sign the confession he was handed by police because Detective Myles told him that he could keep him from getting a death sentence if he signed the paper. (Smith, 1986)

JEROME BOWDEN'S HISTORY

Oral and written statements had been taken from many who knew Bowden. Then Patricia Smith wrote a history to show how unlikely a killer Bowden really was. She described a small, undernourished aimless person with retardation, who just seemed to hang out around the neighborhood. He couldn't make a go of school, couldn't hold a job, couldn't solve problems, and just couldn't make his own way as most people do.

On the other hand, neighbors and friends talked about his soft-spoken pleasant disposition and his respect and willingness to help older people. He also liked being with younger children who needed his protection and care. Folks saw him always trying to look at the bright side of things and always trying to make friends. Those close to him lovingly called him Pa Pa. Some highlights I picked up from Smith's biography of Bowden and the many written statements she received:

- Bowden entered a world of brutal poverty. His mother, age 40, not having the money for a hospital birth, delivered her son in a small frame house in the African American section of Columbus. He was preceded by his half-sister Shirley. Both were illegitimate by different fathers whom they never knew. These two children were preceded by four half-brothers and a half-sister who had already left home. The mother and the two children usually survived on donations and commodities from relief agencies. Shirley recalls a diet of powdered milk and eggs, rice, lard, and Spam. She also recalls living in houses with no electricity or running water, and chopping wood for the stove and fireplace. They transported water to the house in jars and cans. When Jerome was small, he suffered asthma attacks, and others stayed up all night with him because the hospital was too expensive. Because the mother worked away from the home in the early years, the two children were often left alone with an adult looking in on them occasionally.

- School for Jerome was bleak and frustrating. Old records show that in his first year, he was present 96 days and absent 83. All his days were spent in special-education classes so colorless that one teacher stated in a note that she felt her students "were cheated." Another called the education "ridiculous." Still another described how damaging it was to the self-esteem of Bowden and his classmates when, as teenagers, they attended isolated classes in a junior high school. He dropped out of school at that time.

- When Bowden received a psychological evaluation at age 14, the examiner said he received "a full-scale IQ of 59 on the Wechsler Intelligence Scale for Children." He found Bowden undernourished and small for his age, with "off-set ears" which slightly detracted from his overall appearance. Said the examiner, "Jerome's responses to the Rorschach were extremely limited but in keeping with one who is intellectually functioning at the lower limits of mild retardation. He has little or no insight into his situation. . . . He is easily distracted and has a tendency to act on impulse regardless of the consequences." The examiner also made it clear that "he is of course not psychotic."

- Jerome served as an object of ridicule with kids his own age. A neighbor tells the following story:

I knew Jerome Bowden because he worked delivering groceries from the Auten's Grocery Store. I think Mrs. Auten hired him to help him out because the other boys in the neighborhood used to complain that she should have hired someone with some sense. Before I knew him, I heard boys talking around the neighborhood, calling him crazy and retarded. People used to tease him, but it didn't seem to bother him. He didn't understand. He thought they were paying him a compliment when they called him crazy.

● He struggled with disorientation:

I know he had a problem because when he brought my groceries from the store, a block and a half away, he would get lost and wander around for a long time. Sometimes I called several times to find out about the groceries and Mrs. Auten would just tell me he was on his way. When he finally got here with the groceries, he would say something like, "I know where your house is, but I just got lost."

● Bowden was arrested for minor crimes and moved in and out of the local juvenile home several times during his teenage years. One incident described by a neighbor illustrates the connection between his mental difficulties and his crimes:

One time he took some money from Mrs. Auten, but it seems like someone may have put him up to it because he didn't seem to know what he was doing. He didn't try to hide it. I don't think he meant to keep it. I think maybe he just forgot to turn it in, because he was just standing around with it in his pocket when they came looking for it. This is why I don't think he really made the decision by himself. He was easily influenced by others.

● At age 20, he received a five-year sentence for burglary. When the system released him at age 23, he returned to his gentle, roving, always smiling, lackadaisical life in Columbus.

● He stayed with many different relatives and friends. While he was with his oldest half-sister, Josephine Henderson, he borrowed a pair of platform shoes that belonged to his niece, Linda Jenkins, and wore them to a rock concert. He saw nothing strange about what he had done. Henderson remarked, "Jerome's mind just used to come and go." One telling example appeared in Patricia Smith's biography of Bowden:

One day he was cutting Josephine's grass with a power lawnmower. When the mower ran out of gas, Jerome filled it with water from a hose in the house. . . . Then he just walked away and returned a couple of days later. (Smith, 1986)

● Bowden's vulnerability was extremely obvious just before his arrest. Said Smith, "It was in this [vulnerable] situation that Jerome was sought by Jamie Graves. Both Linda Jenkins and Josephine Henderson remember that Jamie, whom Josephine characterizes as 'very smart,' came several times looking for Jerome." His vulnerability continued even after the crime. After Graves implicated Bowden, the police came to Henderson's house looking for him. When Jerome finally appeared at the house, Henderson told him the police were looking for him. Bowden left and found a patrol car at Church's Chicken on Hamilton Road. He walked up to the car and said, "Are you looking for me?"

BOWDEN'S UNDERSTANDING OF DEATH

Based on her work with Bowden, Smith drew the following conclusions:

Jerome is at a very interesting level of mental retardation. He was smart enough to know that he wasn't learning what others were in school. He is smart enough to know that he is different. But he is not smart enough to know that his reasoning ability, his ability to think, is flawed. Therefore, he thinks he is making decisions when all he is doing is mimicking those around him.

Jerome has no real concept of death. He has seen a dead person in a funeral home, and he has walked through a graveyard, and his mother died. But he has no personal understanding of his own existence or of what his nonexistence or death would be. He has been told that dead people cannot hurt you, but his concrete level of thinking still envisions the dead as people. Nonexistence is an abstract concept that is beyond his ability to understand. (Smith, 1986)

The Atlanta Journal, in its June 21 editorial, reinforced this issue strongly:

[Bowden's attorneys] report that some time ago, when his appeals appeared exhausted, the state began its death-watch ritual. It moved Bowden to a cell without access to television. At the last minute, a stay came through. But when a jubilant attorney rushed to inform his client, Bowden could only stare blankly. "Does that mean I can watch ['Hill Street Blues'] tonight?" he asked.

Never mind for now the larger debate over the propriety of the death penalty. The question here is narrower: Should Georgia execute a man who cannot understand what is happening or why it is happening?

Punishment? That is impossible when the person to be punished can't fathom the lesson. Deterrence? It is absurd to think that other folks with problems similar to Bowden's could grasp the warning implicit in his electrocution.

At bottom, the execution would serve no purpose. That is a point on which opponents and proponents of the death penalty should be able to agree.

THE ELEVENTH HOUR

Monday, June 23. In the morning, Irwin Knopf, chairman of Emory University's psychology department, tested Bowden for three hours and presented his report to a waiting Georgia Board of Pardons and Paroles. In the afternoon, the board withdrew the stay of execution. This made it possible for the state of Georgia to execute Bowden before his death warrant expired the next day at noon.

Board chairman Wayne Snow stated that Bowden was not psychotic, not a sociopath, and fell very close to mentally retarded. But Knopf's testing report said that Bowden had "a verbal IQ of 71, a non-verbal IQ of 62 and a full-scale IQ of 65." Knopf added that Bowden would need an "IQ of 45" or less to be spared and sent to an institution for persons with retardation. A paragraph from the board's report:

The State Board of Pardons and Paroles has reviewed said case and petitioner's application; and the Board has reviewed results of psychiatric testing in 1981; and we have also had our own psychologist, Dr. Irwin J. Knopf, interview the subject and the Board has met personally with Dr. Knopf to receive the results of his test and his impressions of Mr. Bowden; the Board has met with the Assistant District Attorney Doug Pullen, who prosecuted the case as well as the District Attorney Bill Smith, of Chattahoochee Circuit, receiving their comments relative to the demeanor and the statements of the subject as he appeared in court and before the jury as well as the testimony of the subject. As a result, the Board finds that Mr. Bowden knew the difference between right and wrong at the time of the commission of the crime, that he knows the nature of crime, and that he has a good vocabulary range. (Georgia State Board of Pardons and Paroles, 1986)

The execution was set for 10:00 A.M. the next day, Tuesday. At 4:00 P.M. Monday afternoon, Bowden was transferred to a holding cell 35 feet from the electric chair. The defense attorneys moved quickly to place a motion before the U. S. Supreme Court. Attorney Smith gave these statements to the press:

That is probably the most unprofessional job I have ever encountered by a professional. No professional in the field gives one test and makes an assumption on one test. It is not done. (*The Atlanta Constitution,* Tuesday, June 24)

This is not a psychological profile that any professional I have ever known would be willing to put his name to (*The Columbus Enquirer,* June 25).

From Bruce Harvey, one of Bowden's defense attorneys:

This is kind of outrageous, we think. We're at the very, very end of our rope. They've given us 18 hours—and just one working (business) hour—to get something up to the Supreme Court.

I talked to Wayne Snow, and he said he'd mail us the order. I said, "Great—the guy'll be dead by then." (*The Marietta Journal,* June 24, 1986)

Statements from Fred Steeple, spokesman for the Georgia Department of Corrections:

He's scared; he understands what's going on. (*The Marietta Journal,* June 24, 1986)
For his last meal, Bowden requested a regular prison breakfast of eggs, bacon, toast, grits, orange juice, and coffee. (*The Atlanta Constitution,* Tuesday, June 24)

Tuesday, June 24. Jerome Bowden was pronounced dead at 10:13 A.M., eight minutes after the electrocution began and thirty minutes after the U. S. Supreme Court rejected a frantic final appeal.

Interestingly, in one of Jerome Bowden's last telephone calls to his attorneys, he discussed the IQ test he had taken a few hours earlier. He told his lawyers, "I tried real hard. I did the best I could."

CHAPTER SIX

BOWDEN'S LEGACY

Picture seven uniformed guards escorting a small, quiet, 33-year-old African American man into the room at 10:00 A.M. on June 24, 1986. Picture him being strapped into the wooden electric chair, while eleven witnesses watch through a plate-glass window.

Picture that man in earlier years as he tried to make a skateboard out of old rollerskate wheels and pieces of wood—as the other kids did—then becoming frustrated and walking away.

Picture him as he opened a book—as his sister did—feeling confused, and going off by himself to curl up in a corner and rock. Picture a young boy so hungry to be an accepted and loved member of the human race, and so unable to figure out how to do it, that he copied anyone around him who seemed to have succeeded.

Now picture the warden saying his ritualistic piece as required by law, then putting the microphone close to Jerome Bowden's mouth and asking if he had any last words. Think how many times Bowden must have wanted to give intelligent recitations—as other kids did—in school and at clubs and before religious congregations on special days. Now, while sitting strapped in a chair, came his first and last chance to give words to the world. They came in three measured, calmly spoken sentences:

I am Jerome Bowden and I would like to say my execution is about to be carried out. [That figured, after all the people who had tried to tell him what was coming.]

I would like to thank the people of this institution. [That was vintage Bowden. No matter what, try to say something kind!]

I hope that by my execution being carried out, it will bring some light to this thing that is wrong. [That sentence threw people for a loop. It was transferred from the witnesses to newspapers and broadcast throughout Georgia. Even columns and editorials were written about what people thought Bowden meant.]

Bowden died, but the issues he represented would not.

June 25. George Kendall, the death-penalty lawyer for the Georgia chapter of the American Civil Liberties Union, in *The Atlanta Journal,* called the action of the state Board of Pardon and Paroles "an ambush."

One of the defense attorneys, Bruce Harvey, told *The Columbus Enquirer,* "The Board of Pardons and Paroles choreographed this to give the appearance of fairness."

June 28. Defense attorney Smith refused to fold up and fade away. In an article in *The Atlanta Constitution,* she said:

> There was something very wrong about the execution this week of Jerome Bowden—something that strikes beyond the age-old arguments surrounding the morality or efficacy of the death penalty as a suitable punishment or an effective deterrent. . . .
>
> People with mental retardation, particularly those in the mild to moderate range, spend most of their lives trying to pass for normal. They have a variety of stratagems. They mimic those around them—the speech, the vocabulary, the walk, the dress, the behavior. They think that if they can do it well enough, no one will notice they are different.
>
> Bowden got so good at it that it killed him. . . .
>
> Mental retardation is not simply something that is measured on an IQ test. Whether someone knows right from wrong has very little to do with IQ. A person whose IQ is less than 45 can be taught this concept. A person whose IQ is more than 100 may never have learned it. The significant variable is that people with mental retardation are much less likely to learn the values of society by osmosis than are persons with a higher IQ. . . .
>
> The purpose of the existence of clemency is to take into consideration the human element, the extenuating circumstances. . . . What is the excuse of the Board of Pardons and Paroles for not understanding its role in our system of justice? Where is our sense of humanity, and what purpose was served by Bowden's death?

July 1. "State Stumbled in Bowden Case," said the headline in a July 1 editorial in *The Atlanta Constitution:*

> Ultimately, the difference between life and death for Jerome Bowden boiled down to a few tiny numbers—IQ points toted up by state-paid professionals. It was Bowden's misfortune to have scored 65 on an IQ test June 23. The state might have spared him had his score been around 45. . . .
>
> Its reasoning was grievously faulty. Whether Bowden understood his fate or not, whether he knew right from wrong—he was indisputably handicapped. . . .
>
> Most states have progressed beyond the dated right-wrong standard in weighing such cases. Most look at a case in which sanity or IQ is an issue and ask: Could the defendant help himself? There is compelling evidence that Bowden could not. . . .
>
> But never mind—it's tough luck for Bowden. Two more days might have made a difference. Twenty points shaved from his test score might have done the trick. Instead, brute whimsy was given full sway. For the state of Georgia, it was a willful lapse of decency.

July 5. Magdaleno Rose-Avila, of Amnesty International, raised incisive questions in *The Atlanta Constitution:* "Why wasn't Bowden's attorney allowed to have a neutral psychologist test him? Why was Bowden hurried into the electric chair?"

July 9. By this time letters to the editors justifying Bowden's execution had appeared in many Georgia newspapers. One example appeared in *The Atlanta Constitution:*

I am so tired of reading about "poor ol' Jerome Bowden." Only two people conceived him and only two people were responsible for him. So he was mentally retarded. So are thousands of citizens, and they don't go out murdering. I could sure sleep better at night knowing "Old Sparky" was working overtime.

The old cliche, "If you want to dance, you must pay the fiddler," holds true for each citizen. Let's quit trying to make the world feel guilty for Jerome Bowden and all criminals and put the blame and punishment where it belongs—on criminals.

I am not my brother's keeper.

October 13. Attorney Doug Pullen, the man who prosecuted Bowden in the 1976 Columbus trial, made it plain to *The Atlanta Journal* that his viewpoint had not changed:

I'm a sucker for repentance. There's a difference between someone who's sorry he got caught, and someone who's sorry for what he did. As a prosecutor, I know defendants who are genuinely shaken by their crime. Here, the guy [Bowden] never once said, "I'm sorry."

On the same day, Board of Pardons and Paroles spokesman Silas Moore announced that the board had received 360 letters of protest—the largest number ever received on a single case. Fifty-one came from outside the U.S.

One woman from Germany said, "I was very frightened that this mentally retarded man was put to death. It reminds me of the history of my own country and a time in which the retarded were also murdered. . . . Please try to explain to me why this man had to be executed" (Montgomery, 1986).

January 5, 1987. Georgia State University unveiled the results of a survey which showed that 66 percent of the state's citizens no longer believed retarded persons should be put to death. The survey carried out by GSU's College of Public Affairs and funded by the Clearinghouse on Georgia Prisons and Jails was presented at a Georgia legislative hearing.

Attorney Smith responded to the survey: "I think what it says more than anything is that a very large part of the population is beginning to have a real good understanding of what mental retardation is all about."

But Wayne Snow, chairman of the State Board of Pardons and Paroles, defended the board's actions: "We will not acknowledge the fact that Jerome Bowden was a severe case of mental retardation. . . . That's just not the information that we had" (Thompson, 1987).

January 10, 1987. Tom Teepen, of *The Atlanta Journal,* followed with a column that explained the survey, then offered an interesting conclusion: "From this fascinating poll, it seems clear that most Georgians are prepared to think practically about crime, the penal system, punishment, and other basic justice issues. Perhaps one day the people will get politicians who can catch up with them."

The protests continued at high pitch for more than twelve months.

February 15, 1988. A Georgia House subcommittee heard chilling accounts of Bowden's death. Pastor Randy Loney described Bowden's last days: "It was the cruelest thing I have ever witnessed in my 40 years on this planet."

Bowden's sister Shirley Thomas described her brother's mental functioning to spellbound legislators. And as she had done on other occasions, illustrated her views by describing the water-hose-in-the-lawmower incident of years ago.

Bowden's attorney Smith—still on the case—testified that people with retardation are "at a tremendous disadvantage" in the criminal justice system because they often do not understand their basic rights. To execute a person after lengthy litigation which the defendant cannot fathom "is probably the most unjust thing I can think of."

The hearing was occasioned by a bill presented by Representative Charles Thomas (D-Temple), at the request of ARC/GA. The bill would bar Georgia juries from imposing the death penalty on persons with retardation by creating a new "not guilty by reason of mental retardation" verdict and a "guilty but mentally retarded" plea (Thurston, 1988).

April 8. Governor Joe Frank Harris signed a bill approved by the General Assembly in March that banned the execution of persons with retardation. In an article in *The New York Times* (April 11), Clive Stafford Smith, an Atlanta attorney who had researched the legal status of persons with retardation while defending such a person, said he knew of no other state with such a law.

In the same article, Georgia Attorney General Michael Bowers, who had opposed an earlier version of the legislation, said the final product was "progressive and a step forward in explicitly recognizing we are not going to impose the death penalty on persons who are mentally retarded."

Fulton County District Attorney Lewis Slaton did not voice the same approval: "What we've always been concerned about is that we are leery of changing the law because it means that every person on death row can now raise another ground."

April 15. *The Atlanta Constitution* lauded the breakthrough in its editorial—then credited it all to the Bowden case:

> Not only did Georgia's Legislature pass a bill to limit the application of the death penalty. Not only did the governor sign it last week. Now the state's strongest critics *and* proponents of capital punishment are hailing the measure as "progressive."
>
> For once, they're both right. If such wonders persist, Georgia might shake its reputation as one of the nation's blindest and harshest backers of the death penalty. What a relief it would be to unload that nasty burden. . . .
>
> The new law is nothing short of remarkable. Georgia's fondness for capital punishment is legendary. Since 1930, we have executed more prisoners (373) than any other state. In the latest census of death-row convicts (done in 1986), Georgia ranked fourth nationally, behind the vastly more populous states of Florida, Texas, and California.
>
> But perhaps it was our very zeal for the death penalty that ultimately brought us to this new posture of restraint. Two years ago, the state executed Jerome Bowden, a mentally retarded man convicted of murder. . . . As he was led to the chair, he made a confused statement that seemed to thank the state for taking such good care of him.
>
> It was an ugly spectacle that unsettled more than a few persons in government and law enforcement.

One year later, the governor of Maryland signed a similar bill banning the execution of people with retardation; within the next two years, the governors of Kentucky, Tennessee, and New Mexico did likewise, and other states are now considering such options.

February 22, 1990. Some legislators remained unhappy with the law and did their best to weaken it. On this day, however, *The Atlanta Constitution* wrote a hard-hitting editorial:

> Two years ago, the Georgia General Assembly enacted a reform that did its members and the state credit. It forbade the execution of the mentally retarded. The change was moderate, sensible, and decent-minded. It would be hard for anyone to argue with.

Hard, but not impossible. Proposals have cropped up in this year's Legislature to repeal the reform or to amend it into pointlessness. They are unworthy.

Legislators are being tempted into regression . . . to discredit it by miscasting how it actually works. (The opponents, disappointingly, include Sen. Pierre Howard, who has fudged on the legislation he supported two years ago. Mr. Howard, perhaps not coincidentally, is running for lieutenant governor.)

This law . . . turns no one loose; defendants convicted under it are sentenced to life in prison. But it does honor one of our society's most deeply embedded values: People cannot be held fully accountable—and certainly not mortally accountable—for acts that they are unable to comprehend. That value deserves the state's protection.

CHAPTER SEVEN

MANEUVERABLE IQ NUMBERS AND DEFINITIONS

Three psychological statements helped to kill Jerome Bowden. While considering an old evaluation done on Bowden at age 14, the trial judge paid little attention to the "full scale IQ of 59," but made much of the statement that Bowden was *not psychotic*. Therefore, assuming no insanity, he opined that Bowden knew the difference between right and wrong. Upon that assumption, he talked the two young court-appointed defense lawyers out of their requests for an up-to-date psychological evaluation and a hearing on whether Bowden was competent to stand trial.

When the state-paid psychologist performed a rushed, three-hour examination on Bowden for the state Board of Pardons and Paroles, he came up with a "full-scale IQ of 65, a non-verbal IQ of 62—and especially a verbal IQ of 71." People don't need to sit in on such cases very long before they realize what goes on in the minds of officials when an IQ score—even a subordinate one—exceeds 70.

The psychologist for the board also mentioned that if Bowden had an "IQ of 45" or lower, he would be excused from execution and sent to an institution instead. That statement led the board to believe they were dealing with a 25-point margin of error.

These statements raise some vital questions.

Are psychological evaluations received differently in the courts than in clinics? Most of the time, psychiatrists and psychologists present their reports to teams of workers in institutions, clinics, and community services, where the people are struggling to help other persons achieve a richer and fuller life. They only want to help, and if the reports are a little off base, no matter. It's usually not worth arguing over. They just keep working with the person.

But the court setting is remarkably different. A veteran attorney who has participated in three thousand trials, including 285 for first-degree murder, puts it this way:

Our justice system is a contest between two lawyers as to which one can tell the biggest lie and manipulate the truth. A jury trial today is supposed to be a search for truth, but it's not. And the jury

39

knows it. . . . Lawyers today will do anything, will say anything to win their case. To them the end justifies the means. And the higher the fee, the more bizarre their tactics become. (Rubin, 1989)

In all fairness, some attorneys, judges, and juries do not fit this mold. On the other hand, when expert witnesses give their opinions in a courtroom, one can observe the defense and prosecution attorneys compressing or stretching the reports as if they were made of rubber. The defense will use them to persuade a jury to understand a defendant and see his or her humanity. The prosecutor, however, will use the same report to show the defendant as evil and subhuman. The more the defendant can be portrayed as a nonperson, the easier it is for the jury to decide on a long imprisonment or death.

Bear in mind also that if a defendant is accused of killing a mother or father of five, a teenage basketball hero, or a child, the audience in the courtroom will be filled with relatives and neighbors who already possess a need to finger *someone*. And the jury, the judge, and the attorneys feel pressure from such an audience.

Presenting a psychological report in this setting is a far cry from reporting to a small friendly circle of human-service workers.

What's so important about an IQ of 70? In some people's minds, that number has become the legal dividing line between persons with retardation and those without. In some death-penalty states, if the jury is convinced that the defendant's IQ is 71, the person can be executed. If the score is 69, the person can be spared. If the defense lawyer can convince the jury that the test bears a 5-point margin of error, the person in question might slip by with a 75.

If someone has an IQ of 76 but a much lower adaptive behavior (skills needed to adapt to the surrounding environment) the person can be executed. On the other hand, if someone has an IQ of 62 and adaptive behaviors akin to people with IQs in the 80s, the person will be spared the death penalty. In some death-penalty states, of course, it won't matter what the IQ may be. Courts in different areas of the country will play down or play up an IQ according to their own whims and desires.

If you find this confusing, you're not alone.

What about people who have a borderline IQ? Until 1973, the American Association on Mental Deficiency (now known as the American Association for Mental Retardation) considered anyone with an IQ between 71 and 85 as being retarded. (The scores, of course, could be hedged up or down a few points, depending upon the percentage of error on certain tests.) (AAMD, 1973).

The AAMD saw the removal of that borderline population as a wise and kindly act. It meant that thousands would never again suffer the stinging stigma of the label *mental retardation*. Without the label, many people in the 15-point buffer zone thrived and passed into the mainstream of the human race. On the other hand, some didn't—especially those with low adaptive behaviors. The label was gone—but so was the financial and professional support. Brandeis University's Gunnar Dybwad recalls the decision and explains the predicament:

Let me say that this was a very touchy subject. What you desire for one person will be unfair to another. For one person it was important that we no longer forced upon them the protections and the accompanying label *mental retardation*. And yet other people—for good reason—needed this protection and support.

For example, a young man who is well-liked in the workshop moves out on his own and gets a job in a government office. He dresses nice—shirt and tie and all—and does his job well. His co-workers like him because he is so accommodating. But if that same man commits an offense or—and this is important—is *accused* of committing an offense, he will accommodate the police by making a confession.

So this guy possesses the same trait in both situations, and we say, "This nice guy who works so well on the job, it would be a shame to call him retarded." But should he get arrested, we say, "Hey, this guy is retarded; he can't adequately defend himself." (Dybwad, 1991)

So helping agencies don't like to call people *retarded* when they have an IQ in the borderline area. And prosecutors, too, refuse to call them *retarded*—but for different reasons.

Is the current definition of mental retardation helpful to courts? Here is the definition which experts recite in courtrooms across the land:

Mental retardation refers to significantly subaverage general intellectual functioning, existing concurrently with deficits in adaptive behavior and manifested during the developmental period. (AAMD, 1983)

Apply a readability test to those words, and you will learn that the reading-ease score will be in the "extremely difficult category." According to one test, you will need more than sixteen grades of school to begin to understand it, and only 5 percent of U. S. adults will understand the definition exactly (Houghton-Mifflin, 1985).

Quite often the experts on the stand fail to clarify that *general intellectual functioning* is based on one or more intelligence tests; *significantly subaverage intellectual functioning* is defined as IQ 70 or below; *adaptive behavior* focuses on how well individuals meet the standards of personal independence and social responsibility expected for their own age and cultural group; and *developmental period* means the period of time between birth and the 18th birthday.

Small wonder the eyes of judges and juries turn glassy when this definition is recited! Professionals in the field of mental retardation have yet to come up with an accurate and clear definition that courts can work with. Until they do, attorneys will treat this formal definition as if it were made of India rubber. Its vagueness allows them to dream up their own definition—one that meets their personal needs.

Do prosecutors argue that defendants are faking mental retardation? You bet they do. Attorney/special educator Ruth Luckasson has been involved in many cases when prosecutors, judges, and a few misguided defense lawyers did just that. She collected their statements and presented them before an audience of lawyers:

He can't possibly be retarded . . .
    . . . because he doesn't drool.
    . . . because you can see how normal he looks.
    . . . because he's so big.
    . . . because he's so mean. (Some feel a person with retardation could never be mean.)
    . . . because he's black and I'm his lawyer and I'm so liberal. (There is a suggestion that to even think that your African American client has retardation is in some way racist.)
    . . . because he played cards with the police officers who bring him over in the van, and one day he won.
    . . . because he can write.
    . . . because he can draw.
    . . . because he can do some things better than other things.
    . . . because no one knows it.

. . . because I asked him and he said he's not, and he started crying.

. . . because I talked to his family and they all denied it.

. . . because I can talk to him easily. He's one of my favorite clients. He does everything I want him to.

. . . because he tried to cover up his involvement in the crime.

. . . because I know he's mentally ill. (You can have more than one disability.)

. . . because he talks so much.

. . . because I saw in his file that ten years ago someone gave him an (unidentified) IQ test, and he had an IQ of 86. (As if that one number clears it up for all time. Of course, that's wrong. I've discovered several people with genuine mental retardation who had in their file some place a relatively high score. The last few found like that had been administered by some mysterious person who used the old World War I Army Beta test [a picture test for draftees who could not read or write]).

. . . because he can drive a car.

. . . because we know he's competent to stand trial.

. . . because he knows right from wrong.

. . . because he's so street smart.

. . . because he can operate a fork lift. (Luckasson, 1990)

Luckasson presented three reasons for this behavior:

First, there seems to be a large proportion of the population who will say, "I'm not sure what the definition of mental retardation is, but I know it when I see it." They just move on their own prejudices and look no further. Second, even very good lawyers—because of financial or personnel resources—have not had true mental retardation evaluators and true mental retardation experts. They have been deceived by certain sections of the psychiatric and psychological professions—or by physicians. So they make conclusions that are not grounded in fact. Third, 90 percent of persons with mental retardation don't drool, don't stumble, aren't mute. They have significantly impaired intellectual ability, but often don't have any physical stigmata that indicates mental retardation. They vary in their skill level. There are some things they can do well and some they can't do well. They are complex human beings who cannot be reduced to a flat IQ test and therefore have the same disabilities in all areas. They won't "look" a certain way. (Luckasson, 1990)

What about measuring adaptive behaviors? This is an ideal way to look at a person—by focusing on a person's effectiveness in self-care, communication, social skills, self-direction, use of leisure time, use of the community, and especially the working and independent-living skills. These tests attempt to compare a person's skills with those of other people the same age and in the same setting.

But judging from the way people talk about adaptive behavior on the witness stand, these measurements are much more complex. One can't put a reliable number on a person's actual adaptive functioning. Also, most of the accepted adaptive-behavior examinations were perfected on people living in institutions, not in the community. Experts often talk about adaptive behaviors on the witness stand, but it's not easy to explain these complexities to judges and juries.

CHAPTER EIGHT

A SUDDEN CHANGE IN THE LIFE OF JOHNNY LEE WILSON

or twenty years, Johnny Lee Wilson lived a warm, well-protected life in Aurora, Missouri—until a fateful Sunday in 1986. Before that day, almost everyone in this small southwestern Missouri town of 6,340 knew this shy, mild-mannered young man with the contagious smile. Even though his father had left home before he was born, Wilson's mother, Susan, and his grandmother, Nellie Maples, more than made up the difference in love and support.

The Aurora public schools adjusted to Johnny Lee's "organic brain damage and mental retardation," provided him with special-education classes, and helped him follow his own rate of development for twelve full years. A principal and special-education teacher who knew him throughout those school years described him as "quiet, reserved, respectful," "never a discipline problem." After graduation, Wilson had sporadic lawn-mowing jobs to which his mother drove him.

Even investigators of the murder of 79-year-old Pauline Martz found Wilson likable. According to Missouri Highway Patrol Sgt. J. J. Bickers, "He was a nice kid. He was polite—yes sir, no sir. He was easy to talk to. The only problem is, he killed her" (Whitley, 1989).

Sunday, April 13, 1986. According to the family, Wilson and his mother and grandmother attended morning services at First Presbyterian Church. At noon, a friend came over and stayed until Wilson was driven to a lawn-mowing job by his mother. She picked him up a couple of hours later. Wilson's friend returned and the grandmother watched a Disney TV program with the boys; then the boys taped songs until supper time. After supper, Wilson and his mother drove to the post office and Ramey's Supermarket. Leaving Ramey's, they heard sirens and followed the fire trucks to the home of Pauline Martz. They then went home to tell the grandmother that the home of Martz was burning; Martz was one of her card-playing friends. Then they returned to the fire.

Monday, April 14. Joplin Police Lt. Dick Schurman called local officers and told them about

Chris Allen Brownfield, a Joplin native who had escaped from an Oklahoma prison. Schurman said that Brownfield "has been known to tie up and beat old ladies and is more than capable of murder" (Whitley, 1989).

Tuesday, April 15. Officers questioned Wilson in his home. Earlier, they had received a tip from one of his former special-education classmates who claimed that Wilson had said he killed Martz. The police background check on the informant revealed a reputation as a chronic liar and troublemaker who had often used tall tales to attract attention. Their former special-education teacher corroborated these facts.

Friday, April 18. Wilson was watching a movie in the Princess Theater when officers came for him and took him to the police station. He was interrogated from 9:30 P.M. until after midnight.

Saturday, April 19. By 1:00 A.M., a confession for the murder of Martz had been signed by Wilson. According to the audiotape, Wilson at first vigorously denied any involvement: "I wasn't near that house. . . . I was with my mom all along. I was at Ramey's with her." The officers ignored his statements of innocence. They assured him that they were his friends, that they wished to help him, and they told him it was okay to "tell the truth." Later, when Wilson failed to tell them what they wanted to hear, the officers accused him of the crime:

Investigator:	You can swear to God or whoever you like, that ain't going to get you out of trouble.
Wilson:	Uh huh.
Investigator:	For you are in serious trouble right now. Murder is what you're in. Murder! Premeditated, willful, malicious, burning up an old lady in her house! That's what you're in on, Wilson. Ain't no sense kidding around about it!
Wilson:	I wasn't near that house though.
Investigator:	I think it's despicable! (*Wilson* v. *State of Missouri,* 1991a, pp. 10-12)

Later, CBS correspondent Connie Chung asked Wilson why he had finally admitted the crime. He said he did it because he felt threatened by the police who "grabbed my face and turned it toward them." He told Chung, "A cop said, 'Well, if you confess,' you know, or 'tell us you did it,' or something, 'we can all go home.' At that point I thought he meant me, too." Excerpts from the officers' audiotape:

Deputy Seneker:	We have the fact that you're the one who started the story about the lady being tied up and in there and gagged before we even knew it, before we'd even found the body! We didn't even know she was in there when you knew it!
Wilson:	And I didn't know it.
Deputy Seneker:	Oh yes, you did! And we can prove it!

Seneker asked about the color of the victim's blouse:

Wilson:	I'll say it was white, kind of white or bluish blouse.
Deputy Seneker:	Okay, how about bluish? I'll go for that.
Wilson:	Yeah.
Deputy Seneker:	How about bluish-green, maybe.
Wilson:	Yeah.

Still later, Seneker asked what, besides a rope, was around the victim's ankles.

Wilson:	I'm thinking.
Deputy Seneker:	What are some things that could be used?
Wilson:	Handcuffs, I think.
Deputy Seneker:	No. No. Wrong guess. (CBS TV, 1990)

Mrs. Martz' ankles had been bound with duct tape.

April 15, 1987. A competency hearing was held. Psychologist Daniel Foster and psychiatrist William Logan, representing the defense, claimed Wilson was not competent to stand trial because of brain damage, mental retardation, and a dependent personality disorder. Fulton State Hospital psychiatrist Mahinda Jayaratna, psychiatrist for the prosecution, stated in a written report that Wilson was competent. The judge ruled in favor of the prosecution.

April 30, 1987. Wilson pled guilty to first-degree murder and was sentenced to life with no parole. Wilson was led repeatedly by the judge. One example:

Judge Elliston:	You understand that the State has a strong case and that you could very possibly get the death penalty imposed upon you if you had a trial in this case. Now, what's your understanding of why you're here this afternoon?
Wilson:	Plead guilty.
Q.	Why are you pleading guilty, Johnny?
A.	I don't know.
Q.	Pardon?
A.	I don't know.
Q.	You don't know why you're pleading guilty?
A.	Just for first-degree murder.
Q.	Well, that's what you're pleading guilty to, but why are you wanting to enter the plea?
A.	I don't know.
Q.	Do you want to enter a plea of guilty?
A.	Yes.
Q.	Why do you want to enter a plea of guilty?
A.	(No response.)
Q.	You can go ahead and talk to me.
A.	I don't know.
Q.	Do you know that the death penalty is a possibility in this case?
A.	Yes.
Q.	Do you want the death penalty?
A.	No.
Q.	Do you want to avoid the death penalty?
A.	Yes.
Q.	Are you admitting that you committed this murder?
A.	Yes. (*Wilson* v. *State of Missouri*, 1990)

February 1988. Kansas State Penitentiary prisoner Donald Waymire wrote to Missouri officials, stating that fellow inmate Chris Brownfield had killed Martz. Brownfield—the man Lt. Schurman had called about the day after the murder—was now serving a life sentence for robbing and murdering an elderly woman in Pittsburg, Kansas, sixty miles northwest of Aurora—just sixteen days after Martz was killed. Brownfield stated later that he had told Waymire to write the letter so he could collect a reward. When that didn't happen, Brownfield said he couldn't let a person with retardation take a rap for him and told about a stun gun he had lost in the violent room-to-room ransacking of the Martz home; the fire had been set to destroy the fingerprints on the gun. (The police had found a stun gun in the ashes, but had made no public statement about it. When police showed it to Wilson, he thought it was an electric shaver.)

April 26, 1989. When Wilson appeared in the county circuit court, he said he hadn't committed the crime. June 27 was set for a hearing on the motion. When Brownfield offered to appear, the hearing was reset for July 27, but Brownfield refused to appear because Missouri failed to promise a life sentence instead of the death penalty. At the hearing, the prosecution attacked the credibility of Brownfield's admissions, and the judge overruled the motion for a trial. Later, state public defender William J. Swift entered the case and claimed that the prosecution had withheld evidence consistent with Brownfield's admissions that would have cleared Wilson.

September 12, 1990. In Springfield, Wilson's relatives and neighbors, along with local reporters, jammed the Missouri Court of Appeals, and forty people were turned away. At the hearing, defense attorney Swift appealed to the court to vacate Wilson's plea of guilt. Swift based his arguments on (1) Wilson's impaired development; (2) his activities on the day of the crime; (3) the police investigation; (4) the competency hearing and Judge Elliston's conduct therein; (5) Chris Brownfield's admission of responsibility; (6) Wilson's responses at the plea hearing; and (7) his inability to consult with plea attorneys in a meaningful fashion. Swift's conclusion:

> Unquestionably, Ms. Martz was the victim of a terrible crime. There is, however, another victim, a mentally retarded young man, whose only mistake was his handicap which caused him to confess to a crime for which there is substantial evidence it was committed by Brownfield. (*Wilson* v. *State of Missouri,* 1990)

Assistant Attorney General Elizabeth Ziegler argued that Wilson's guilt or innocence did not matter in this hearing. The court's decision, according to her argument, would focus on whether the legal procedures had been conducted in accordance with the laws of the state—no more and no less.

November 14, 1990. The court ruled against Wilson, claiming that he had known what he was doing when he pled guilty. The court also felt that Brownfield's admissions of guilt were irrelevant; it ruled that newly discovered evidence does not afford a basis for postconviction relief.

LOCAL AND NATIONAL EFFORTS KEEP HOPE ALIVE

Wilson has entered his fifth year in the penitentiary without ever having a trial. State and local law enforcement officials continue to insist that they arrested the right man for the murder of Pauline Martz. So much time and such solid belief by law enforcement officials usually grinds advocacy efforts to a halt. In this case, however, the efforts continue to keep up the pressure.

  • Relatives and neighbors of Wilson refuse to fade away. Spearheaded by former next-door neighbor Dean Rodgers and resident Warren Ormsby, the group members attached FREE JOHNNY WILSON BY TRIAL bumper stickers to their cars and erected billboards that expressed the same sentiment.

● Dustin Toler, a former dispatcher in the sheriff's department, came forward with a 14-point fact sheet showing how officials mismanaged the case and covered up their mistakes. Toler—who has a brother with retardation—also related that officers used derogatory terms to refer to Wilson:

> "The sheriff often referred to him as slow," said Toler. "Others referred to him as moron and dumb sh—t. By cutting him down, that would make them look bigger. That's just part of their mentality. [Others] referred to Wilson as a "f——— retard." (Maurer, 1990a)

Toler resigned shortly after the investigation.

● Roughly 2,600 residents signed petitions seeking an inquiry into the investigation of Martz' death. One group even walked the 157 miles from Aurora to Jefferson City and discussed the case with representatives of the governor and attorney general. The attorney general did send officials to investigate, but they concluded that the investigation had been handled in a proper and professional manner.

● The Free Wilson movement continues to face vicious opposition from law enforcement officers and some town officials. Even so, the movement and its dual leaders remain tough and vocal. Johnny Lee Wilson's mother and grandmother—still bewildered by all that has happened—lean on Ormsby and Rodgers for advice and representation. In a recent telephone visit with Grandmother Maples, she recited her litany about Johnny being with his family all day—a litany she feels she must give to all visitors. Then, as usual, she referred all other questions to Ormsby and Rodgers: "Thank goodness for them. I just don't know what we'd do without them."

● On November 11, 1990, *Unsolved Mysteries* presented the story of Wilson on NBC's national television feed. Auroran Lucille Childress, age 74, who watched the program, felt she could not keep silent any longer. She contacted the *Marionville New Press* and told them she had seen Wilson and his mother at Ramey's on the night of the crime:

> I stopped in at Ramey's to get some things. Johnny and his mother were in there. I came out right behind them. But while I was in the store, we heard the fire sirens blowing. We came right out. The mother said, "Johnny, let's take our groceries home and go see where this fire is." (Maurer, 1990b)

Childress explained later that she had kept silent because she feared her relatives would be harmed.

● Since three major television networks produced features on Wilson's predicament, the controversy has widened. Letters of protest now flow to Jefferson City from all over the United States and from foreign countries. For example, a group of self-advocates in Omaha, Nebraska, viewed the story of Wilson on CBS-TV. Feeling that the same thing could happen to their own members, they circulated petitions and sent them to Missouri governor John Ashcroft. The president of Project II, Ollie Webb, wrote to the governor:

> Dear Sir:
>
> I am writing you on behalf of Project II regarding Johnny Lee Wilson. Project II is a local self-advocacy program in Omaha, Nebraska. Self-advocacy is speaking out for yourself and for the rights of those persons who have a disability and who can't help themselves. In this case I am speaking up for Johnny Wilson.
>
> Project II doesn't believe he committed the crime and we want you to review the facts of the case and release him from prison.
>
> Enclosed you will find 300 signatures of people, not just self-advocates, but parents, family members, professionals and interested citizens who agree with Project II.

Please release Johnny Wilson with a full pardon. Let him return to his home and try to forget the wrongs that have been done to him. (Webb, 1991)

The governor replied that the case was out of his hands. According to him, it must be decided by the Missouri courts (Launderville, 1991).

● Jefferson City song writer Linda Powers, after learning of Wilson's plight, visits him regularly and also transports his mother and grandmother for visits. These relationships moved Powers to write a country and western ballad, "We All Want Johnny Home," which has been distributed to individuals and radio stations throughout the state, and concerned groups across the country:

This Johnny Lee Wilson thing
Keeps tugging at my heart.
Right now I don't know what to do
Or even where to start.
They say he killed a woman
But he was with his mom.
They say he set a house on fire
Don't you know that's wrong.

Chorus:
What happened to this young boy?
They threw him in a jail.
He never got a trial or out on any bail.
And the thing that I keep hearing
On TV and radio
We don't believe he did it
And we all want Johnny home.

A man over in Kansas
To this crime confessed.
The reason that he did it
Is anybody's guess.
He knew things about that woman
The killer could only know.
So why is Johnny behind bars
Scared and all alone?

A retarded boy in prison
Somehow that don't seem right.
Until he gets his freedom
We'll all put up a fight.
Against the courts and system
That's put him through this hell.
We've got to join together
Get Johnny out of jail.
(Linda Powers, © 1990)

NEW STIRRINGS IN THE STATE SUPREME COURT

On May 9, 1991, the Missouri Supreme Court heard the case in Jefferson City. Again Public Defender Bill Swift argued the case. This time, however, his efforts were supported by an amicus curiae ("friend of the court") brief submitted by the American Association on Mental Retardation under the signatures of four attorneys—James W. Ellis, Barbara E. Bergman, Charles W. German, and M. Elizabeth Kirkland.

In a surprise move, a former Kansas attorney and former candidate for governor, Vern Miller, managed to obtain a recording of Chris Brownfield, the self-confessed killer of Pauline Martz, talking to his alleged accomplice. Miller, now in private practice in Wichita, arranged for Brownfield to be transported from the prison in Lansing to Wellington in southern Kansas, where he made telephone contact with the alleged accomplice. Miller delivered the transcript to the AAMR lawyers, who relayed it to Swift. One hour before the supreme court hearing, Swift submitted the document to the justices. Excerpts from the transcript:

"We need to talk," said the alleged accomplice.
"All right," said Brownfield.
"You've been talking too much for my likes, brother."
"Well, I didn't start off talking about nobody, except just myself."
"Well, you finished off talking about everybody."
"Well, I run into a situation to where when I got to confessing to that Marks deal."
"Well, why did you do that?"
"Well I started out doing it, cuz I didn't have no money. I was going to collect the reward off the deal. Now I found out they got some retarded kid that they done benaggled around and . . ."
"You knew that."
"Huh."
"You already knew that."
"I knew they had arrested somebody, but hell I didn't know they convicted him."
"We read it in the paper."
[Later:]
The alleged accomplice said, "I've seen you on TV, I've seen the whole deal, I heard the whole deal . . . You know, all this s—. You know, I have your voice on tape telling all about the deal. Yeah, I heard your voice."
"Yeah you heard it."
"Yeah I did."
"What was I supposed to do, _____, leave the kid laying in there like that?"
"Why not?"
[Still later:]
"So I said well I ain't gonna say who was with me, and they said well if you don't, how we supposed to turn this kid loose and if we can't verify nothing? After about an hour I finally said, well _____ was with me."
"Well thanks, God damn. It took you a whole hour to cop me out." (*Johnny Wilson* v. *State of Missouri*, 1991b)

This surprise submission to the Missouri Supreme Court stimulated spirited questions from the justices about whether the governor could issue a pardon, or whether this court could indeed consider new evidence. Public Defender Swift was ready for such questions, but Assistant Attorney General Ziegler held to her usual argument that new evidence cannot be admitted. Although she received the surprise brief at the same time the justices received it, she said she didn't have time to read it.

Although the alleged accomplice never actually stated that he had taken part in the murder of Martz, it was enough to convince Miller that an injustice has been done: "There is no question in my mind that Chris Brownfield and [the other man] committed that murder, and there is absolutely no question in my mind that Johnny Lee Wilson is innocent." He criticized Missouri Attorney General William L. Webster, saying that a similar investigation could have been done in Missouri: "I don't know if it's because of politics or what, but the investigation of that case was one of the worst I've ever seen" (Ganey, 1991).

The Missouri Supreme Court has yet to hand down its ruling. In the meantime, Assistant Attorney General Ziegler holds fast to her beliefs that Wilson's plea of guilty was credible and not forced and that new evidence cannot be introduced. And Doug Seneker—now a lieutenant in the county sheriff's department—continues to stand behind his interrogation of Johnny Lee Wilson:

> There have been a zillion people I've sent away (to prison) that made up their mind they didn't like it once they got up there. This is the most vocal appeal process I've gone through, but it certainly isn't the first one. It'll pass like the rest of them. . . . There is a principle in interrogation. A person will not admit to something they haven't done, short of torture or extreme duress. No matter how long you're grilled, no matter how much you're yelled at, you're not going to admit to something you haven't done. (Davis, 1990)

CHAPTER NINE

"FRINGE" PEOPLE, YET?

During recesses in the retrial of Johnny Paul Penry in Huntsville, Texas, July 2-17, 1990, people with varying views mingled and slowly learned the reasons for one another's attendance. It didn't take long for folks to know I wrote about people with mental retardation. That fact got me all kinds of mentors. For example, a patrolman-turned-investigator gave me his views:

"As a patrolman, I saw myself as part of the town's sanitation department. My job was to cruise the streets and keep an eye on the garbage of humanity."

"Where do you find them?" I asked.

"They live in different parts of the town. They're the fringe people."

"Fringe people?"

"Every town has them. They didn't know it, but I watched and waited for my chance. And the first time they broke the law, I got them off the streets."

At this point, my questions seemed to be getting in his way. So I just listened. It soon became clear that the fringe people he talked about were any "strange-acting" people—usually retarded, or poor, or ethnic, or any combination of the three. He understood that "some of the better people" had family members with retardation as well. He did not doubt, however, that if they ever moved away from the control of their families, they too would become part of the criminal element in town.

Several of America's most prominent educational researchers in the first three decades of this century would have agreed wholeheartedly with that investigator. Stephen Jay Gould, in *Mismeasure of Man,* documented how Lewis Terman, Robert Yerkes, Henry Goddard, and C. C. Brigham attempted to identify and exclude certain people from the mainstream of society. They did not use the terms *garbage* or *fringe,* but they still equated intelligence with virtue—and feeblemindedness with criminality (Gould, 1981, pp. 146-233). Goddard, in the last chapter of *The Kallikak Family,* made it clear that these "loathsome unfortunates" needed to be rounded up and kept in "colonies." He also mentioned "the lethal chamber" as an option, but he feared society would not yet tolerate such a practice (Goddard, 1916, pp. 101-17).

CHAPTER TEN

A NEAR-MISS FOR WILLIE BENNETT

On the morning of October 24, 1989, all Boston learned that "an urban savage" had cut down "a starry-eyed couple out of Camelot." It had happened the night before, as they drove through the African American community of Mission Hill. According to Charles Stuart, the husband, an African American robbed them, shot them, and ran. Carol Stuart, pregnant and near to term, received a bullet in the back of her skull. Charles received one in the stomach. Bleeding and not sure of his location, he called for help on their cellular phone, and a calm police dispatcher worked out a system for zeroing in on the car. The tragedy exploded as a media event when the ambulance arrived with a television crew on board.

In the days that followed, the media portrayed the couple as one of Boston's best. Governor Dukakis, Mayor Flynn, and Cardinal Law attended Carol's funeral. A love poem written in the hospital by Charles and read in the service melted hearts. The *Boston Globe* glorified the couple, calling their relationship "a shining life." Seventeen days later, the death of the baby taken from the dead mother only heightened the emotion.

So warm-hearted love and concern flowed toward Charles Stuart, and a white-hot hunger for revenge floated over Mission Hill—until it settled on 39-year-old William Bennett. Hundreds of investigators scoured the Mission Hill community for the killer until Bennett became their prime suspect. As bizarre as it may seem, the police never arrested him—yet the whole world knew he was being interrogated and that they were working night and day to gather evidence against him.

By New Year's Day 1990, politicians began to groom Bennett for the death chamber. This, of course, meant that the state first needed to legally reinstitute the death penalty. But that was in the works. The day after the tragedy, Republican party chairman Ray Shamie had called a press conference and, with great feeling, called for the restoration of the death penalty in Massachusetts. Shamie had never called press conferences after any of the scores of other murders in Boston that year, the vast majority of which were white on white or black on black.

More incredible, according to Robert Turner in *The Boston Globe* on January 7, "Not only did [District Attorney Newman] Flanagan jump on the capital-punishment bandwagon in October, he directed an investigation that focused public attention more on a series of [African American] suspects than on discrepancies in Chuck Stuart's story."

Early on the morning of January 4, when the nation's feeling for Stuart had reached its peak and Bennett seemed doomed, Stuart jumped off a bridge. It was Stuart who had killed his own wife and unborn child.

Stuart's splash doused powerful emotions, but the steam of bewilderment, guilt, and blame that emerged afterward proved just as powerful. The media bashed politicians, and politicians bashed back. Ordinary citizens—not used to bashing everyone at the drop of a hat—seemed to silently carry the anguish until it dissipated and the case became distant history.

But something else that proved interesting emerged in Mike Barnacle's January 7, 1990, article in *The Boston Globe*. Apparently, the police had picked up the school records of Willie Bennett. Barnacle printed what the police had found:

> Bennett did not finish the seventh grade. He dropped out of the Timilty School in 1964. Then, the Boston public school system listed his verbal IQ at 64, performance IQ at 65, and a full-scale IQ of 62. Stamped on his academic record is the following term: MENTAL DEFECTIVE. Here are the marks off his last report card issued that November.
> Conduct: E
> Effort: E
> English: E
> Math: E
> History: E
> Science: D
> Geography: D
> The E does not stand for excellence. [In that school, E stood for failure.]

The way Barnacle used Bennett's school records makes one wonder whether the spirit of Henry Goddard and his term *loathsome unfortunates* might be making a comeback.

More important, one wonders how the prosecutors would have used these test scores in Bennett's trial. Bennett was already African American and poor—and possibly vicious. Would that label *mental defective* make him even worse?

Then another bit of information was furnished. Philosopher Hugo Adam Bedau at Tufts University decided to look for concrete ways to heal the breaches and learn from them:

> Will anything be learned from the murder of Carol Stuart? That depends. If the pattern of fear continues to be the matrix into which new information must fit, little will be learned. The cycle of death will continue.
> On the other hand, if that pattern begins to unravel—if reality refuses to fit that matrix—then some of the lessons of this tragedy may hit home. (Bedau, 1990)

Bedau reinforced his point with an example:

> About two months after her murder, Carol's family, the DiMaitis, announced the creation of a foundation to support college scholarships for the minority youngsters from Mission Hill, the area where the murder occurred—a gesture meant to help compensate for the harm done by Charles' false implication of an African American man from that neighborhood.
> By this act, the DiMaitis have reminded us all that efforts to build lives, not destroy them, are an essential part of any civilized response to death, including murder. (Bedau, 1990)

CHAPTER ELEVEN

DID EARL WASHINGTON TRY TOO HARD TO PLEASE COPS?

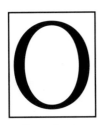n June 4, 1990, in Richmond, Virginia, two attorneys who work with no fee, claimed that a man with mental retardation followed the "leading" of investigators so well that he was sentenced to death for a crime he did not commit. Defense attorneys Eric M. Freedman and Robert T. Hall stated before the 4th Circuit Court of Appeals that 30-year-old Earl Washington, Jr., did not rape and murder Rebecca Lynn Williams in Culpeper, Virginia, on June 4, 1982—exactly eight years earlier.

Freedman, arguing the case before a three-judge panel, claimed the conviction was based solely on a confession whose details were supplied by police. Judge J. Harvie Wilkinson III asked if Washington's role was "purely a passive role . . . or did he actually supply concrete details about the perpetration of this crime?"

"It was purely passive," said Freedman.

"Are you saying he had words put in his mouth?" asked Wilkinson.

"That's what I'm saying, Judge," said Freedman. But he added that he didn't believe police were trying to railroad Washington. He said they simply may have believed Washington was holding out on them (Green, 1990).

Freedman and Hall described the situation in their written preliminary statement (*Commonwealth* v. *Washington,* 1990). Rebecca Williams, who had been raped and stabbed, was found lying in the doorway of her apartment and died two hours later at a local hospital.

According to the police, a witness reported seeing a man near the Williams apartment on the morning of the murder. He was described as "a black man with a beard," dressed in a white sleeveless T-shirt and faded blue jeans. He had "extra large muscles in the chest, arms and upper back areas." That description did not fit Washington, although it did fit a suspect who had been arrested shortly after the murder, but was interrogated and released.

One year later, on May 21, 1983, Washington was arrested in Warrenton, twenty miles northeast of Culpeper, for assaulting his brother-in-law. His arrest came in the morning after he had been up all night. He had been drunk, and yet, according to the defense, "Washington, mentally retarded with an 'IQ of 69' and sleepless the night before his arrest, was interrogated at great length that day and the next."

Although the initial charges were dropped, Washington "waived his Miranda rights" and "confessed" to a number of other crimes, including the rape of a Warrenton woman. After initial investigations, all officials concurred later that he could not have committed any of those local crimes.

An officer's notes, taken late in the first day of interrogation, state, "Earl still seemed nervous as though there were still something else being kept from us." After some probing, the officer spoke bluntly: "Earl, did you kill that girl in Culpeper?" Earl "shook his head yes and started crying."

Later the officer asked, "Earl, I mean the woman you stabbed in Culpeper?"

Washington answered yes. (He made no mention of rape. Even the officer didn't know at the time that the woman had been raped.)

During later interrogations—with Culpeper police taking part—Washington usually proved to be wrong any time he volunteered facts:

• He told them Rebecca Williams was African American. The officers corrected him. She was white.

• He said she was "kind of short." She was 5'8".

• He said he kicked in the door. The door wasn't damaged.

• When asked how many times he stabbed her, he wasn't sure—perhaps one to three times. She was stabbed 38 times.

• He said nobody else was around. Yet police who arrived shortly after the event found a baby in a playpen just inside the door; standing beside the playpen was the victim's three-year-old daughter.

• While his confession was being typed, officers drove Washington to apartment complexes throughout Culpeper. When they arrived at the crime scene, Washington failed to point it out. They drove away, and then came back, but again Washington failed to point to the apartment where the crime had been committed. They drove away and returned a third time. This time, an officer said "Earl, isn't that the place?" He said yes.

Freedman and Hall also cited forensic evidence that excluded Washington as the killer:

• Seminal fluid stains on the bedding where the rape had taken place and seminal fluid and blood found in the victim's vaginal vault did not match that of Washington. It did possess characteristics of the first suspect.

• Several months after the murder, a shirt was found in a dresser drawer at the scene and thought to be related to the attack. Blood spots were found on the shirt. According to police, Washington said it was his, even though ten Negroid hairs and hair fragments in the pocket were consistent with hair from the first suspect—not from Washington.

• Numerous fingerprints were found throughout the apartment, but none matched Washington's.

• The eye witness was never brought to the court proceedings—even though he or she provided information to the police which had led to a composite drawing.

The defense in the earlier trial had received no psychiatric or psychological assistance in the preparation of the case, though when they asked the court for an examination, a three-psychiatrist committee was appointed. But the committee reported it was "unable to determine with reasonable professional certainty Mr. Washington's competency," so the court ordered another examination at Virginia's Central State Hospital. A professional at that institution claimed that Washington was competent to stand trial and testified later for the prosecution that Washington did understand his Miranda rights.

On habeas corpus appeal, the new defense utilized Dr. John N. Follensbee, former chief Army psychiatrist for Europe. In his affidavit, Follensbee attacked the conclusions of the professional from Central State Hospital, stating that the wrong test had been used to check for the process of organic brain damage. There was a 90 percent probability that Washington had "in fact suffered from organic brain damage."

The affidavit also stated that Washington did not understand his Miranda rights: "Mr. Washington not only did not understand the point of the police advising him of his rights, he did not understand the concept of rights—a concept which requires very little capacity for abstraction." He also said that the stress caused by a sleepless night and long interrogations "would have induced a condition of absolute compliance and utter reliance on the interviewer for appreciation of results."

"Earl Washington is mentally retarded and can't tell you the colors of the flag, or what a thermometer does," said Freedman, "but he has been sentenced to death. . . . He's simply innocent . . . retardation doesn't only mean you don't know things. It also means you try and conceal [retardation]."

Follensbee's affidavit showed how Washington compensated for his condition:

> This man is easily led. Out of his need to please and his relative incapacity to determine the socially and personally appropriate behavior, he relies on cues given by others and a reflexive affability. These are his only apparent adaptive skills. It was my impression that if, on the evening of his execution, the electric chair were to fail to function, he would agree to assist in its repair. (*Commonwealth* v. *Washington*, 1990)

"The jury didn't know anything about the scientific evidence," Freedman said. "They didn't know Earl would have said yes to anybody. Nobody explained that he would have signed a statement to be cooperative. They didn't know he [falsely] confessed to another rape" (Brown, 1990).

Washington's first attorney, John W. Scott, told the current lawyers that he hadn't appreciated the "importance of that information." Because he is now a judge, Scott declined to comment, other than to say he believes Washington is innocent (Brown, 1990).

Linwood T. Wells, Jr., of the Virginia attorney general's office discounted the importance of the defense's recent evidence. He felt the confession was too solid (Green, 1990).

A juror in the first trial nevertheless clings to his earlier decision: "I felt like he did the crime even though they are trying to say he [would have] confessed to anything. I think [police] did it straight. I have to feel that way because you have to have faith in policemen" (Brown, 1990).

The 4th Circuit Court of Appeals has yet to rule on whether Washington will be executed or given a new trial.

CHAPTER TWELVE

THE EVER-TIGHTENING SYSTEM

T he criminal justice system often functions like a ratchet. After an arrest, officials move a defendant through various stages (e.g., interrogation, arraignment, indictment, bail, pretrial hearings, etc.). With each movement, the system clicks, moving a person down a one-way path, deeper into the bowels of the system. The more often the system clicks, the harder it is for a person to get out. Sometimes the clickings occur more quickly when the defendant possesses retardation or similar disabilities.

Therefore, if officers have misunderstood the detained person's responses, the sooner the misreading is clarified, the better. After all, the further officials go in building their case, the more egos and territories become involved—and the more faces must be saved if they are wrong.

Former Alameda County, California, prosecutor John Taylor describes the situation:

> There certainly is selective perception in law enforcement. The police and prosecution focus on a suspect, and even if you try not to, human nature is such that you are going to focus on convicting that person, rather than keeping your mind open and believing that you could be wrong. You waste a lot of time when you do that. Statistically, most often you will be right, in the overwhelming majority of cases. (Taylor, 1989, pp. 251-52)

On the other hand, ten years after convicting Aaron Owens for murder, John Taylor discovered leads which showed that the man was innocent. In private practice at the time, Taylor pursued those leads, admitted his error, and voluntarily fought for Owens' release (Taylor, pp. 247-48).

Some find it harder, however, to admit such a mistake. Police officers in St. Joseph, Missouri, had repeatedly picked up, interrogated, and released 25-year-old Melvin Reynolds, a man with retardation. Finally, after six months of such harassment, Reynolds had broken down and confessed to the May 28, 1978, murder of Eric Christgen, age four. Reynolds was convicted and sent to prison.

Four years later, FBI Agent Joseph Holtslag and Prosecuting Attorney Michael Inscho reversed themselves and connected the child's death to serial killer Charles Hatcher.

When that happened, many in the law enforcement community turned on one another. In Terry Ganey's *Innocent Blood,* we learn that some of Reynolds' earlier investigators admitted the error while others did not. Police Chief James Robert Hayes, still insisting Reynolds was guilty, tried to pressure the FBI into relocating Holtslag. He was unsuccessful. So sure of his department's interrogation work, Chief Hayes went to his grave believing that Reynolds was the killer. The parents of the young victim—putting their faith in Hayes and his men—also failed to make a shift in their thinking.

Unfortunately, when Reynolds left the prison and returned to St. Joseph, he faced grim conditions. The argument continued to rage over his guilt; consequently, no one was willing to give him a steady job and because of his disability and poverty, he couldn't move away.

In another situation, the system became tense for David Heilbroner, a prosecutor for New York's Manhattan district attorney. After three highly successful years, he resigned. In *Rough Justice: Days and Nights of a Young D.A.,* he tells how he found himself becoming hardened toward people: "The tiny, human differences between one case and another, details that had seemed so colorful only a few months ago, had become distractions," he said. "Just give me the facts; things are busy."

In the end, the lies got to him. Heilbroner felt that everybody lied—cops, witnesses, doctors, even victims—even though they had sworn to tell the truth. Then he began to feel sympathy for defendants. Knowing, however, that feeling sorry for them "had no place in the prosecutorial mentality," he left the job (Heilbroner, 1990).

CHAPTER THIRTEEN

WERE WALTER CORRELL'S FIRST LAWYERS TOO APOLOGETIC?

A wild drug spree went out of control shortly after midnight in Roanoke, Virginia—and the court case that followed seemed just as bizarre. On Sunday, August 11, 1985, shortly after midnight, John Dalton, Richard Reynolds—and possibly Walter Correll—met drug pusher Charles Bousman. After they had ingested the man's drugs, things got out of hand and they stabbed him to death with his own knife. Later, Dalton and Reynolds told police that Correll was the "ringleader."

Correll is 5'6" and 130 pounds, has mental retardation ("an IQ of 68, the mental age of a 12-year-old"), a history of backing off from any kind of violence, and has generally been known as "a wimp."

Correll received an uncommonly brief trial and a subsequent sentence of death on May 5, 1986. Recently, three lawyers—Michaux Raine III of Rocky Mount, Virginia, as well as Joseph D. Tydings and Robert E. Pokusa of Washington, D.C.—have picked up Correll's defense at no charge. In a January 30, 1980, writ of habeas corpus, they list particulars to show that Correll received an incredibly ineffective defense:

- The defense attorneys failed to do any preparation, conducted no investigation, failed to help Correll receive a jury trial, and ignored mitigating factors related to mental retardation in the sentencing hearing.

- The formal court records show that Correll's trial lasted roughly four hours, with the 193-page trial transcript containing only 18 pages of the four defense witnesses' testimony. The 3-hour 114-page sentencing hearing contained only 35 pages of testimony from defense witnesses. In the summation of that hearing, one of the defense attorneys offered an interesting apology to the jury:

> I was in a bar meeting in South Boston and came back and was advised by the Court that Ms. Jamison had been appointed to represent Mr. Correll and so had I. After going through [the prosecutor's] case I wasn't real excited about it but Ms. Jamison talked me into it and we agreed to go forward. (*Correll* v. *Thompson*, 1989)

● The extent of the defense attorneys' investigation consisted of meeting the prosecutor and finding out what they had against their client. Then they opined that Correll was guilty—in spite of Correll's repeated claims of innocence throughout all the hearings.

● In a hearing on an alibi, one attorney told the judge:

Mr. Correll, myself, and Ms. Jamison have debated whether or not he has an alibi. *He has what he thinks are alibi witnesses.* I cannot tell the Court that we are going to present an alibi defense; we might. In that light, I will tell him who the witnesses are if you so direct. (*Correll* v. *Thompson,* 1989)

● That attorney admitted to an inability to communicate with the client during the sentencing hearing:

I went down and I talked to Mr. Correll, and the same frustration I think the Court has about his inability to talk about the offense has bothered me. I think it is the same frustration that the social worker had that worked with him. When you talk to Walter about what happened, as Dr. Showalter [a psychiatrist called for the defense who never mentioned the IQ of 68 on the stand] said, he goes into a shell that has three parts: One, I don't think I was there because Cissy's parents said that I was with them part of the time; Two, hopefully God will help me; and Three, I am going to kill myself.

Both Ms. Jamison and I were trying to get Walter to either focus on the night in question or on why he confessed to Billy Overton [the police investigator]. He just went into a shell; he would curl up in the corner and he would cry and it did get frustrating. . . . [It] was very hard to get Walter's attention. . . . I am convinced that for whatever reason that Walter confessed because probably he was there and he thought getting it off his chest would make things better and the next thing he knows they come back and say, "Thank you, Mr. Correll: now, we are going to attempt to execute you," and I think that pushed him right back in his shell. (*Correll* v. *Thompson,* 1989)

● Just prior to a hearing on Correll's right to a trial by jury, Correll met to discuss the possibility. The defendant expressed his desire to be tried by a jury. Counsel, however, informed him that if he did not waive his right to a jury trial, he would be convicted and receive a death penalty.

● Counsel knew little or nothing about mental retardation, and no attempts were made to research and learn for the sake of the client.

A conflict remains over whether Correll was at the crime scene at all. Friends of Dalton and Reynolds say he was. Others claim they saw him at other times during the evening, making it almost impossible for him to be present at Bousman's killing. Correll claims he can't remember anything about that night because he had already ingested alcohol and drugs from other sources.

The new attorneys, after research, claim that Correll, though unarrested, was literally a personal prisoner of one of the investigators. For hours, Correll claimed he couldn't remember anything that happened that night. Then slowly but surely, after long hours of protestations, Correll was allegedly fed facts about the case by the investigator. Finally—as many people with retardation have done—he figured that the only way to stop the awful pressure was to give the investigator what he wanted. He confessed.

Raine, Pokusa, and Tydings have begun to move the case through the formal appeals processes, hoping for a new trial. As for their commitment to the cause, "The three of us are in this one for the duration," Pokusa said.

CHAPTER FOURTEEN

HORACE BUTLER AND HIS $300 DEFENSE

Ten years ago, Horace Butler, an African American 22-year-old man, received a quick, haphazard trial and a death sentence for the rape and murder of a white convenience-store clerk. But the trial has been followed by ten rounds of appeals over whether the trial was fair. Today, both the current prosecution and the defense personnel look at the case and shake their heads—each, of course, for different reasons.

Appellate attorneys John Blume and David Bruck claim that Horace Butler, now 31, faces execution because of an incompetent defense lawyer. The lawyer received $300 for his services but spent a mere ten minutes telling the jury why Butler should not be put to death. The jury based its verdict only on Butler's confession, unaware that the man "had an IQ of 61," because the trial lawyer had not had him tested. The jury was never informed of the man's clean police record.

The prosecution laments the many appeals that keep the man from being executed. Cases like Butler's forced South Carolina's senior senator, Strom Thurmond, to sponsor legislation for "streamlining and shortening the appeals process." According to him, it's not fair for a victim's family to suffer year after year, waiting for a killer to die. The senator also declared that his constituents are fed up with procedural loopholes and judicial delays that keep condemned criminals out of the death chamber.

The crime: On June 17, 1980, 18-year-old Pamela Lane ended her day of work at Dodge's convenience store outside Charleston at 10:00 P.M. and was riding the fifteen miles to her sister's home on her new moped. She never completed the trip. According to a coroner's report, Lane had recently had intercourse, then had been shot in the chest with a .22-caliber gun and thrown off a bridge. Early on the morning of September 1, police began to question Horace Butler about the crime. After he waived his right to remain silent, the officers interrogated him all day and all night, and by 5:45 the next morning, possessed a signed typewritten confession.

The actual facts of the case appear to be so scattered and convoluted that the prosecution admitted having doubts about even trying Butler. And the lack of an energetic investigation and defense made it worse. Even so, Butler did receive a death sentence on January 26, 1981. He could be the fourth person to die on death row in South Carolina since the reinstatement of the death penalty.

Recent Reflections on the Case (Marcus, 1990):

● Trial prosecutor Steve Schmutz, reflecting on the case: "If I would have known Horace Butler was mentally retarded—if he was—I would not have sought the death penalty on him."

● Current Charleston County Solicitor Charles Condon stated that he had won seven death sentences, but, "They don't get killed. So for all of the energy and the resources we put in to prosecuting these cases, the appeals system, I think, makes a mockery of it. To me, one of the safest places to be in South Carolina is on death row."

● Scharlette Holdman, an investigator for Bruck and Blume, doubted whether any harm accrued to the people of South Carolina from the delays in the Butler case: "Horace Butler was safely locked on death row. . . . The harm truly is irreparable when we execute people because of an arbitrarily imposed time limit on fairness."

● Bruck claims the issue is whether "you want to sacrifice people who are innocent or who don't deserve the death penalty, so you can execute the Ted Bundys faster." As for Butler, Bruck felt the case shows how blindly and randomly the death-selection process chooses just a few of the large number who commit homicide. "Only a handful of the most badly represented, the poorest, the most retarded, and the most unlucky are sentenced to die."

In the summer of 1990, the South Carolina Supreme Court ordered a new trial. The date of the trial, which will be held in Charleston, has not yet been set.

CHAPTER FIFTEEN

THE PUZZLING WORLD OF JOHNNY PAUL PENRY

ll of us enter this world as tiny defenseless infants, totally at the mercy of the giants orbiting around us. Our earliest years contain hundreds of puzzling little longings and agonies we just can't seem to figure out. Over time, however, we master them. That is, if all those larger, stronger arms around us are good at nourishing and guiding and hugging and protecting. Those arms—and the voices that came to us from beyond them—became predictable and from them, we learned the basic rules for getting along with others.

Johnny Paul Penry never knew such an atmosphere. The second child of his family, he was born on May 5, 1956, into a world that was incredibly unkind. His breech birth was difficult. His 18-year-old mother lost so much blood that the doctor ordered transfusions—which the father, a Jehovah's Witness, refused to allow. She barely survived, suffered a nervous breakdown, and went directly to a mental hospital.

Ten months later she returned home and launched a series of attacks on her son that lasted for more than a decade. According to Penry, as she beat him, she sometimes screamed that she loved him. Records show that he suffered repeated bruises and scaldings, as well as deep scratches and cigarette burns over most of his body. His left arm was broken several times. His head and legs still bear scars. He was locked in a room for such long periods that it became fouled with his own body waste. He was even forced to eat his own excrement (Ellis & Rice, 1988).

When Johnny was two and the Penry family lived in Bacliff, on the Gulf Coast near Houston, Texas, neighbors Betty Olney and Billy Johnson spoke of hearing "terrible, terrible screams" every afternoon. "They weren't like a two-year-old crying or even a baby crying," said Johnson. "They were horrible screams. Terrified screams . . . would just go on and on." When Olney and Johnson mustered up courage to walk into the Penry home and see what was going on, they tried to get police and welfare officials to intervene. But Mrs. Penry threatened to sue and the authorities backed away (Ellis & Rice, 1988).

By age ten, Johnny had developed into a jumpy, short-attention-span bundle of impulses. Professionals caromed him between diagnostic clinics and three state institutions (Texas University Child and Adolescent Psychiatric Division, Galveston; Mexia State School; Austin State Hospital; Rusk State Hospital); and his labels underwent modification at each stop: "Organic brain syndrome with mental retardation and behavioral disturbances," said the University of Texas; "Organic brain syndrome with psychosis due to repeated trauma and mild retardation," was the professional opinion of Austin State Hospital. Psychologists tacked on IQ numbers ranging from 51 to 63 at different times during his institutional career.

Later, his father and aunt (who had recently replaced the divorced mother in the home) took 16-year-old Penry out of Mexia after learning about on-the-ward homosexual activities in which he was involved. He returned with them to Livingston, Texas, where he lived an aimless, impulsive life, his relatives doing their best to supervise him and keep him under control.

At 17, he walked away and shortly afterward was arrested for setting a fire in an apartment he shared briefly with another man. He returned to Austin State Hospital, then transferred to Rusk State Hospital, and at age 18, went back to his family in Livingston. Again relatives did their best to keep him in check. The police began to pick Penry up every now and then—especially for his awkward attempts to interact with women.

At 21, he was arrested and pled guilty to a charge of rape, receiving a five-year sentence at Huntsville. (Interestingly, the victim of that rape took the stand in Penry's last trial and described the earlier attack. Although Penry used force and provoked extreme terror in the woman, she described his awkwardness, sudden loss of tumescence, and even the bluff and bravado that followed. During cross-examination, she admitted she felt sorry for him.)

Parole came early, in August 1979, at age 23, despite a psychological report for the Texas Rehabilitation Commission report which stated:

> [Penry] has very poor coordination between body drives and intellectual control. . . . He also tends to be very defensive and may tend to protect himself from anticipation from hurt from others through aggressive acts.

THE MURDER

Just two months later, on the morning of October 25, 1979, at around 9:30 A.M., Penry rode his bicycle to the home of Pamela Moseley Carpenter. He knocked on the door and asked if her husband was home. He wasn't. He forced his way into the house. What happened next varied, according to defense and prosecuting lawyers. But it was evident that Carpenter had attempted to stab Penry in the back with a pair of scissors. He then beat her violently and allegedly raped her (no rape kit was utilized for forensic evidence), stabbed her in the chest with the same scissors, then rode home on his bicycle.

Carpenter managed to telephone a friend who summoned an ambulance. She died in the hospital at 12:05 P.M.

Hearing about the crime on the police radio, a deputy sheriff drove to Penry's home. Penry agreed to go to the police station and later to the crime scene. At the crime scene, officers said Penry indicated he had committed the crime. Upon returning to the station, officers read Penry his Miranda rights at least three times during the next eleven hours. The officers also stated that they received two confessions from Penry during that period. No audio recordings were made, and officers typed the confessions because Penry cannot read or write. He signed both confessions.

The Agony of a Town and a Trial

Since the key issue here deals with a person who has retardation, most of the descriptions focus on Penry. But if this effort had dealt with the suffering of murder victims and survivors, just as much could have been said about their painful experiences.

Pamela Carpenter, age 22, vivacious and well-liked by everyone who knew her, came from one of Livingston's most prestigious families. Her gentle father, Jack, was a deacon of the church. Her warm, down-to-earth mother, Rossie, could welcome you to the ranch for dinner at a moment's notice. All her brothers were high school football stars. The oldest, Mark Moseley, star kicker for the Washington Redskins, later was named Most Valuable Player of the National Football League. She was known as her brothers' best rooter and once served as co-captain of the high school drill team. National Public Radio's Nina Totenberg summed up the way local people viewed the victim: "In East Texas where football is king, Pamela Moseley Carpenter was a princess" (Totenberg, 1988).

Pamela's death so roused the people in Livingston that the trial was transferred to Groveton, forty miles to the northwest. But to East Texans, a forty-mile drive equates with a city dweller's ten-block walk, so the room was filled as Penry's case went to court. On March 13, 1980, four months and fifteen days after the crime, a jury took only 65 minutes to determine that he was competent to stand trial.

During the trial, the prosecution, to the satisfaction of almost everyone in town, made a quick but strong case. The defense, of course, presented evidence of Penry's childhood abuse, brain damage, and mental retardation.

Even Penry took the witness stand. When he spoke, he sounded cool and knowledgeable—until he was questioned by the defense. Then it became clear that he couldn't read and write (after years of rehearsing, he could sign his name). He couldn't name the days of the week or the months of a year, couldn't count to 100, couldn't say how many nickels in a dime or name the President of the United States (Ellis & Rice, 1988).

On April 1, the jury found the man guilty in just over an hour. The next day, the court met to decide on the sentence. The judge informed the jury that a death sentence needed only a yes vote on three issues:

1. Did he deliberately commit the crime?
2. Was the crime committed without provocation?
3. Will he be dangerous in the future?

It took the jury only 46 minutes to vote yes on all three.

THE U. S. SUPREME COURT INTERVENES

On June 30, 1988, as Penry's execution drew near, the United States Supreme Court agreed to hear Penry's case. The hearing was held in Washington, D.C. on January 11, 1989. The Court considered two issues:

1. Should Texas juries be allowed to consider mental retardation as a mitigating factor when pondering the death penalty?
2. Is it cruel and unusual punishment to execute persons who have mental retardation?

Although it had never been done before, the American Association on Mental Retardation quickly pulled together a remarkable coalition on behalf of Penry. The Association joined with ten other national organizations and submitted an amicus curiae ("friend of the court") brief to the Supreme Court (*Penry* v. *Lynaugh Amicus*, 1988). The brief argued that to execute persons like

Penry was a violation of the Eighth Amendment's ban on cruel and unusual punishment; that death would be a disproportionate punishment because of their impairments; that their disabilities kept them from the required level of blameworthiness; and that the execution of such a person "served no valid penological purpose." In cases like these, it would be "nothing more than the purposeless and needless imposition of pain and suffering."

As January 11 drew near, legal and mental-retardation experts discussed the constitutional and clinical verities of Penry's situation on network newscasts, talk shows, and with reporters from the nation's major newspapers. On the morning of the hearing, the *Washington Post* published a poll by the Louis Harris organization which reported that 70 percent of the American people opposed the death penalty for persons with retardation. Earlier that morning, people—mostly mental retardation professionals—arrived before daybreak, hoping to gain a seat in the courtroom. By 6:00 A.M. the line stretched from the massive front doors of the Supreme Court down the steps to First Street, and around the corner onto Maryland Avenue.

The Supreme Court Hearing

Since the trial defense lawyer had no experience in appellate work, Curtis Mason, drawn from a small pool of lawyers employed by the Texas Department of Corrections, defended Penry before the Court. Though most inmates distrust employees of the same agency that executes them, Mason's thorough brief was accepted for a Supreme Court hearing. Interestingly, Mason went to law school and joined TDC after retiring ten years earlier as a geologist for the National Aeronautics and Space Administration. Mason, however, possessed a quiet professorial demeanor rather than the bearing of a scrappy defense lawyer, and he did not come off well before the justices. Lawyer/columnist Alan Dershowitz described the defense as "a disaster":

> The attorney spoke haltingly and his words were difficult to understand. He seemed not to understand some of the justices' questions. When he did, he frequently gave the wrong answers. He couldn't find needed references. He became so bogged down in technical detail that Justice O'Connor had to remind him, with only three minutes left in his argument time, that he had not addressed the main issue—whether it was constitutional to execute a mentally retarded prisoner. (Dershowitz, 1989)

Dershowitz used the occasion to dramatize the way "hundreds of mentally retarded inmates," already confused and vulnerable, were being represented by lawyers who "are so clearly out of their league." If Penry dies, Dershowitz felt it would be because "he picked the wrong person to kill, he was born to the wrong parents, and the wrong [appeals] lawyer represented him."

The Supreme Court's Verdict

On June 26, 1989, the Supreme Court handed down two sharply divided decisions. It voted 5 to 4 that persons with mental retardation could be executed. Then came another 5 to 4 ruling that the penalty phase of Penry's case must be retried because the jury had not been instructed to consider the mitigating factors caused by his mental retardation.

Justice Sandra Day O'Connor cast the deciding vote in both situations. She justified her vote for possible execution on the basis that the Court could deny the possibility of execution only when a consensus of states legislated such a ban.

Advocates for persons with retardation wondered when the Supreme Court suddenly became an organization for surveying the states instead of interpreting the U. S. Constitution. But they also saw a new legislative goal for each state. At the time, only Georgia and Maryland possessed laws that banned the execution of persons with retardation. Kentucky, Tennessee, and New Mexico were soon to follow, leaving 36 death-penalty states to face the issue at this writing.

Time Magazine, on July 10, published a poll in conjunction with Cable News Network after the Court's decision. The results showed that 61 percent of the population still did not favor the death penalty for persons with retardation.

With the case back in the Texas court, officials could grab an easy out, if they wanted it. They could commute Penry's sentence to life imprisonment with no parole and call it quits. Or they could order a re-trial and go for the death penalty again. They chose the latter.

Also, according to Texas law, the state carried out more than was required by the Supreme Court. All that had been ordered was a retrial of the sentencing portion. Texas, nevertheless, went all the way back to the beginning, to a trial that contained all three phases—competency, evidentiary, and sentencing.

RETRIAL IN TEXAS

The Competency Phase

Huntsville, May 10, 1990—Unlike the celebrated Supreme Court hearing when leaders in the field of mental retardation vied for seats, only the family, the press, and hometown friends of the victim appeared in the Texas courtroom. So without the earlier notoriety, court-appointed Huntsville laywer John Wright sat alone during the competency phase, vigorously defending Penry as he had in 1980. It became obvious that—in spite of the low pay given a defense lawyer—he had spent months preparing the case.

During the recesses, the audience expressed anger over Wright's obvious efficiency. Why did this hometown attorney claim his client could not get a fair trial in Huntsville? Why did he move for a change of venue? What's wrong with Huntsville? (The basic industry in this town with a population of 24,000, 46 miles west of Livingston, *is* the prison business. Eight state prison units are situated within and around Huntsville. Almost all the jury members had relatives in that industry.)

Almost everyone in the audience welcomed one another warmly, and they welcomed me, too, though they knew my reason for being there. Penry, on the other hand, was utterly excluded. In their minds, he had already been written off. They quietly cheered as the prosecutor racked up points with the jury; points made by the defense seemed to have no effect. They handled my brief nods and interchanges with Penry by telling me I was misguided in believing Penry was retarded. After all, the law-enforcement witnesses had said repeatedly, "He may have been a little slow, but I didn't see him as retarded." And prosecutor Joe Price hammered away that "the guy is faking retardation." One relative of the victim busied himself taking notes for a book on the case. "It won't be published," he said, "until the last chapter is in place—the one that describes Johnny Paul Penry's execution."

The competency trial centered on two questions:

      1. Was Penry too retarded to understand the court proceedings?
      2. Was he capable of helping his lawyer prepare a defense?

Highlights in the Defense:

    ● Three death row inmates described how they and a few others had created a circle of protection around Penry.

"I've never known a man in my life that wanted to have friends more than Johnny did," said James Vanderbilt. Penry was so childlike, Vanderbilt and the others said that they functioned like baby sitters. Harvey Earvin explained how Penry's hunger for acceptance had set him up for ruthless exploitation until the circle decided to protect him. James Beathard testified that the circle even tried to keep him away from reporters, "who could lead Johnny and get him to say almost anything they wanted to hear."

• Attorney Curtis Mason described his relationship with Penry while defending him in the Supreme Court: "I talked to him as best I could in one-syllable words. Then [after awhile] Johnny would ask a question, and I saw he didn't understand anything I had been telling him." Mason showed that most of the psychological reports placed Penry in "IQ ranges between 50 and the low 60s." He stated unequivocally that Penry was unable to consult with his lawyer in preparing the case and did not know what was going on in the proceedings: "I didn't rely on him for anything."

• Death-row psychologist George Wheat, who received a subpoena and testified against his will, strengthened the defense by describing his contacts with Penry during the past nine years. He cited a series of incidents showing that "Johnny doesn't compute things like a normal person does."

When asked to rank Penry's intellectual functioning among the other 300-plus inmates on death row, he said, "We have some with IQ 160. But Penry is at the other end with three others. Two of those are smarter than he is. He is in the running for low man."

The prosecution began its case with rapid-fire interrogations of four death-row guards:

Prosecution: "Have you observed Johnny Paul Penry?"
Guard: "Yes sir."
"Have you talked to him personally?"
"Yes sir."
"Did he ever say anything that's crazy, like going to Mars or something?"
"No sir."
"Is he oriented to time and place?"
"Yes sir."
"Have you had any trouble understanding him?"
"No sir."
"Have you seen him communicate with his attorney?"
"Yes sir."
"Have you seen him reading and writing?"
"Yes sir."
"Do you think he has a reasonable understanding of the trial?"
"Yes sir."
"Do you think he understands the proceedings?"
"Yes sir."
"Do you think he has a basic understanding of right and wrong?"
"Yes sir."
"Do you think he can control his own actions?"
"Yes sir."

And so it went with each guard, with small variations. But those leaning in favor of Penry would have felt the prosecution's case was weak—until they heard the last two witnesses:

• It took Dr. Walter Quijano, the former chief psychologist for the Texas prison system, 45 minutes to present his academic accomplishments and explain exactly what a forensic psychologist does. He did it with wit and stage presence—all aimed at the jury. I found myself wondering if we had anyone in the field of mental retardation who could match this guy. Then he launched into his findings.

Penry was "an antisocial personality" with all the symptoms. He was faking mental retardation ("all inmates test up or test down according to the situation"). He showed no remorse. Quijano found him self-centered, manipulative, vicious, dangerous. He placed Penry in the "mild to dull normal range," basing this on a verbal IQ of 72 found in an early Wechsler Intelligence Scale for Children ("this high number shows his potential").

When defense attorney Wright asked Quijano to comment on George Wheat's intellectual ranking of Penry, he responded, "I don't dispute it but I don't believe it." In a subtle way, he made it plain to the jury that his experience and academic credentials far outweighed those of that hands-on cell-block psychologist with only a master's degree.

When Wright asked if perhaps Penry merely tried to appear normal, he replied, "That is true. But we don't have to be retarded to want to look better than we are. That's why we wear clothes."

But doesn't he seem like an outcast among outcasts seeking approval?

"He didn't seem different to me."

But what about all the abuse he suffered?

"There is such a thing as negative grace," Quijano said, "and good things can come out of abuse."

Wright then asked Quijano to tell the court what happened when he and both lawyers got up to leave after Penry's psychological examination.

Penry had asked Quijano, "What do you think of me?"

Quijano had answered that as a psychologist and as a Christian, he had to reply honestly, "Johnny, you are a good person, but you have done wrong things."

When Dr. Quijano was asked to step down, he turned to the jury, smiled, and waved good-bye.

• Dr. Fred Fason, a Houston psychiatrist in private practice, also recited a lengthy list of academic accomplishments, including more than 1,000 competency examinations over a span of 17 years. He also placed Mr. Penry in an IQ range between "mild and dull normal." His overall diagnosis was three-pronged: "antisocial personality, sociopathy, and psychopathic personality—antisocial type." His opinions came after two examinations—one that lasted three minutes and one that lasted twenty minutes. He also felt that Penry was faking retardation. Part of this view stemmed from the fact that Penry called John Wright his *attorney,* when most people use the less-sophisticated term *lawyer.*

The next morning, May 16, prosecutor Price began his closing argument in the competency phase by moving the podium closer to the jury. He began in earnest by attacking the testimony of the three death-row witnesses. Those three, who were basically the same as the defendant, "would make Penry a vegetable, a good-sized couch potato needing a baby sitter." He pointed out that all four were convicted murderers, living together in a common situation.

He felt death-row psychologist Wheat had "a relationship with Penry as a patient, caring for him, and putting that interest first."

As for the guards, "I don't like to brag about the witnesses, but they rub elbow to elbow with 300 of the worst murderers, and they do it without guns."

Focusing on all the institutional records submitted as exhibits, he said, "I look at the records kind of like a photograph that's kind of out of focus . . . different degrees—mild, moderate, severe—25 years of them from different agencies. . . . But the longer you look at them . . . you start seeing a picture . . . you see Penry had the ability to learn . . . you see a nightmare emerging . . . you see that *sociopath* is part of his mental ability."

Defense attorney Wright—a gentle Texan and a member of the society represented in the audience, but strongly committed to Penry—appealed to the jury to "take another look at Johnny

Paul Penry," to notice that though it was not his doing, "Johnny Paul Penry is an outcast among the outcasts—a child in a man's body who has been trapped like an animal."

Then, since this was only the competency hearing—not the trial—he asked them to focus on only that issue—competence to stand trial.

"Will he understand the words the attorney will ask? Will he be able to express facts to his lawyer? I don't think so. We have special ed. in our schools, but we do not have special courts."

At 10:35 A.M. the jury retired for deliberation.

One hour and 17 minutes later, the members of the jury found Penry competent to stand trial. Judge Joe Ned Dean thanked the jury, discharged them, and set May 22 for the impanelling of a new jury for the trial.

The Retrial—Guilt-or-Innocence Phase

The middle phase—to find Penry guilty or innocent—started on July 2. It came after struggling for more than a month to seat a jury acceptable to both prosecution and defense.

Defense attorney Wright was now joined by Robert S. Smith, Judith S. Lieb, and Joseph H. Brennan from the New York office of Paul, Weiss, Rifkind, Wharton & Garrison. They had offered to serve without pay and were accepted. Smith, Brennan, and Lieb also brought with them five paraprofessional volunteers for behind-the-scenes work. No doubt about it, when they joined with Wright, they worked long hours and did superb defense work. But local people in the audience—definitely not on the side of the defense—often spoke with derision about this "invasion of Yankees."

Two area prosecutors, Terry Brown and David Weeks, joined Joe Price at the prosecutor's table.

The procedure tended to be a repeat of the 1980 trial. Many of the same friends, relatives, officers, and clinicians testified. Some of the earlier witnesses had died, and attorneys read their testimony into the record.

On the fifth court day, *Monday, July 9,* the jury went into deliberation and found Penry guilty, after one hour and 32 minutes.

Judge Dean called a day's recess and ordered the sentencing phase to begin on Wednesday. The litigation, which had begun on May 10 and had cost great amounts of time and money, now approached the all-important phase—the only phase ordered by the Supreme Court.

The Retrial—The Sentencing Phase

As if nothing had taken place previously, the defense and the prosecution moved at each other with fresh vigor. These life-or-death arguments counted now as never before. And the court now began to do just what the Supreme Court had ordered in the first place: Consider the mitigating evidence of retardation in deciding for life without parole or execution by injection.

Wednesday, July 11: Playing Down Retardation. Prosecution brought to the witness stand every officer connected with Penry's arrest and interrogation. One by one, they stated that Penry might have been slow, but they didn't think he was retarded.

Thursday, July 12: Extreme Abuse. Defense produced two sisters, a brother, three aunts, a next-door neighbor, and a former baby sitter who provided the jury with a picture of incredible torture. Again, family members described how Penry's mother returned from a mental hospital and began those terrible years of vicious attacks. Again, a neighbor reported that on summer afternoons she had heard Penry, at age 2, screaming "terrible, terrible screams."

Penry's brothers and sisters, because the mother had died, could speak out now without fear of reprisal. They added that the mother used to call Penry "the little bastard," "the little nut," "Blackie Carbon." (Unlike the rest of the family, Penry's hair is coal black and relatives admitted he had been conceived by a man other than the family father.) He still bears scars from scalds and burns. His mother kept him locked in a room—often without food—for long periods. When he couldn't get out to go to the toilet and defecated on the floor, his mother sometimes made him eat it. At other times, after he had urinated in the toilet, she dipped some into a cup and made him drink it. She threatened to cut off his penis for wetting his bed. Once she tried to drown him in the bathtub. Other relatives claimed they knew Penry had been singled out as a special target, but they did not interfere because they too feared the mother.

Thursday Afternoon: Evidence of Mental Retardation and Brain Impairment. Dr. Randall Price, a Dallas clinical psychologist and neuropsychologist, served as the defense's only expert witness. He spent eleven hours testing Penry; using nine of ten tests from the Halstead Reitan Battery, he found brain impairment in eight tests. Using the Wechsler Adult Intelligence Scale, he found that Penry had a "verbal IQ of 63, a performance IQ of 66, and a full scale IQ of 63." He administered tests on faking and found that Penry was giving the best answers he could. Price examined a massive pile of medical records (especially from the University of Texas Medical Branch at Galveston, Austin State Hospital, Rusk State Hospital, and Mexia State School), focusing only on evaluations, not on treatment records, and listed Penry's IQ scores through the years:

	Verbal	Performance	Full Scale
1963 (age 7)			60
1965 (age 9)	55	55	51
1971 (age 15)			51
Jan. 1973 (age 17)			Less than 50
Sept. 1973			50
Oct. 1973	59	74	63
1976 (age 20)			43
1979 (age 23)	56	72	61
1990 (age 34)	63	66	63

The defense presented a large blown up photograph of a single page from a reading test administered to Penry when he was fifteen and living at Mexia State School. It contained pictures of a dog, a door, an airplane, a hen, and a hat. Penry had been asked to underline the one right word out of the five beside each picture. He did underline "dog" and "airplane" correctly. But he underlined "flag" for hat, "drum" for hen, and "dress" for door. The defense used the blow-up to dramatize that Penry could not read or write.

Dr. Price's presentation was long, thorough, exacting, technical, and given as if he were in a professional meeting. It was the right stuff, but one couldn't help noticing three jurors moving uncomfortably while two others struggled to keep their eyes open. Dr. Price tried so hard to give the defense lawyers what they wanted, he may have ignored the need to reach the hearts and minds of the jurors. At the end of the day, it appeared his work was done. He tied things up neatly and the defense rested Thursday evening after his testimony.

Dr. Price probably expected to be excused to return to Dallas. No so. Prosecutor Price requested that Dr. Price (no relation) return for further cross-examination on Friday.

Friday, July 13: The Prosecutors Work on Dr. Price. Prosecutor Price decided to hold the testimony of his expert witnesses until Monday. Then, with the exception of a brief early-morning issue, he kept Dr. Price on the stand almost all day.

Prosecutor Price criticized Dr. Price for reading only the records on evaluation, not those on treatment. Then he and the expert went over every record, one by one, to determine what he had read and what he had not.

Together, they moved through the large piles of old-style medical reports, most of which contained problems and incident reports (e.g., scuffling, running away, pencil and scissor poking, fire-setting, youthful homosexual interactions). Each critical incident was thrown in the face of Dr. Price in such a way that he could only look at the record and admit it was there, all right. Then the man who had come only to report his clinical evaluations was asked such questions as, "Doesn't that sound like an antisocial personality disorder to you?" or "Doesn't that sound like he may be faking?" A seasoned worker with persons having retardation would have responded "no" and "not necessarily" to many of the questions. But as a tester and examiner, Dr. Price seemed at a loss for words.

The prosecutor then hammered away at Dr. Price's findings of brain impairment. Using the same cross-examination method, the expert could only quietly acquiesce when the jury learned that nothing visible to the eye could be found—no holes, no tumors, no lesions or infarctions. The prosecution even presented its own electroencephalograms and brain scans of Penry, which also showed no observable physical damage. As far as the prosecution was concerned, no observable physical damage meant no brain damage.

At the end of the day, the defense attorney read excerpts from reports and letters in an attempt to present Penry as he really was. Again, it was the right stuff, but apparently no one was in the mood to hear it.

Monday, July 16. Prosecution Experts Deny Mitigating Circumstances. At the beginning of the day, defense attorney Smith presented the "litany of abuses" Penry had suffered in his life. It was a devastating list.

Then the prosecution took over. Actually, their strategy had begun a week earlier, just before the summations in the trial phase.

Dr. Fred Fason, the Houston psychiatrist in private practice, returned to the stand, and although the issue had been guilt or innocence, he focused heavily on the two highest IQ scores, the performance IQs of 74 and 72. He told the jury that these represented Penry's highest potential.

"You cannot do better on IQ test scores than what you are capable of doing," he said. "It's like an athlete. You cannot run the 100-yard dash faster than what you're capable of. You can run it slower, however." For this reason, Fason felt Penry tended only toward the "dull normal" range. This vivid word picture—runners doing their best at one time and not doing their best at another time—would have provoked laughter at a meeting of knowledgeable professionals. In the courtroom, however, the doctor planted a seed in the mind of the court that connected with the testimony of the prosecution's last two expert witnesses.

● Dr. Walter Quijano, the former chief psychologist for the Texas prison system, took the stand again to tell the jurors he did not feel Penry was truly retarded. He played down the IQ measurements and brain-impairment tests of Dr. Price and criticized Price for failing to test for adaptive behavior. He also claimed that Dr. Price erred by not administering the Minnesota Multiphasic Personality Inventory (MMPI), a test that examines propensities. Quijano told the jury that Penry didn't have "academic smarts" but he did have "street smarts."

Quijano went on to claim that Penry was an antisocial personality with every symptom listed in the American Psychiatric Association's *Diagnostic and Statistical Manual-III-R* (e.g., grossly selfish, callous, irresponsible, unable to feel remorse or learn from experience and punishment)—the very same symptoms attributed to highly intelligent serial killers like Ted Bundy.

In regard to the litany of abuse Penry suffered as a child, Quijano responded that as a child in the Philippine Islands he had suffered abuse from an alcoholic father that may have been worse than Penry's. Although he did not elaborate, he added, "The abuse made me very determined not to become like my father."

Dr. Stanton E. Samenow, a nationally acclaimed forensic psychologist from Falls Church, Virginia, the co-author of the 1500-page, three-volume *The Criminal Mind* and author of *Children and Crime* and *Before It's Too Late*, took the stand. He told the jury that people probably don't turn to crime because of something outside themselves, but that crime resides within the individual. Therefore Samenow rejected every defense argument that child abuse could be linked to Penry's criminal conduct. After reading records for twenty hours but making no examination, he told the jury that Penry's was a criminal personality "in the extreme sense."

Tuesday, July 17. Summation and Deliberation. Judge Dean's instructions to the jury were similar to those of the 1980 trial. He did add, however, a vital phrase. He explained that mitigating circumstances may include "any aspect of the defendant's character and record or circumstances of the crime which you believe could make a death sentence inappropriate in this case." He also made it clear that all the evidence now rested in the jurors laps and that the following summations would not provide any new items.

Prosecutor Weeks Opens. The prosecutor emphasized Dr. Samenow's statement that there was no connection between the child abuse and the crime. When Weeks ended his summation during the guilt-or-innocence phase, he had fallen to his knees and acted as if he were sitting on the stomach of the victim. He had raised his hands above his head, clutching an invisible scissors, and brought his hands down, screaming, *"He plunged the scissors into her chest!"* Jurors had flinched then, and now they seemed to steel themselves for a similar ending, but it never came.

Smith Sums Up for the Defense. Smith put his hands on the rail of the jury box and spoke softly. Issue by issue, he argued for the mitigating evidence—the retardation and the child abuse.

"This is not the kind of man you kill," he said. With motions and words, he tried to make the jury feel what Penry must have felt. Smith enacted a larger mother, doubling up her fist and beating an infant to the ground. He enacted the mother holding a small Penry under water, shouting *"I'm gonna kill you, you little bastard!"* He wanted the jury to feel what it was like to have their mothers come at them with a butcher knife, or force them to drink a cup of urine or pick feces off the floor and eat it.

"Well, I've got to hope and I've got to believe child abuse like this could give you a different perception," he said. "What does all that have to do with this case? Prosecutor Weeks says, 'Nothing.' It's just a coincidence. Only a really smart man with a really hard heart could say it had nothing to do with this case." He pleaded with the jury to see that some of this guilt belonged to the mother.

"Take some of the guilt off Johnny's shoulders," Smith said. "All I'm saying is give him life."

The end of his summation focused on Penry's "future dangerousness." Smith pointed out that guards wrote Penry up for threatening an inmate with a broken board (a person who had been teasing him). Guards removed two "shanks" (plastic toothbrush handles melted around razor blades) from his cell. But that was early in his incarceration.

"He's not done anything in the past seven years," Smith said. "He is not dangerous in prison. He is one the prison system can handle and has handled." He walked to the defense table, stood behind Penry, and put his hands on the defendant's shoulders.

"This man is a human being," he said.

Price Delivers the Final Summation. This prosecutor now used the very last minutes to refute all the defense's claims.

"The defense talked about Penry having a little boy's mind," Price said. "Does anybody in this jury think he's got a little boy's mind? How many of you think he thinks like a little boy?"

Price continued: "They bring in Dr. Price, and he talks about playing with puzzles. I wonder how long it took him to build those shanks." The prosecutor kept driving: "In the jungle, Penry might be the smartest guy there. But take him out and give him an IQ test, he comes out low. *Nothing says you've got to leave your common sense behind.*"

Penry sat quietly through it all, drawing on pieces of paper provided by his attorneys. Even when lawyers shouted and pointed angry fingers at him, he didn't respond, he just kept drawing. Such was his attitude throughout the ten days of his trial.

The Deliberations. At 12:12 P.M., the jury retired. Penry stood up and turned around with his hands clasped in front of him. He surveyed the audience as he had done so many times during the trial—looking into faces, always quick to smile and nod if anyone nodded to him.

At 2:49 the jury came back. The audience sensed the excitement, but Penry, standing and watching the audience, smiled.

The jury had voted on three special issues after considering the judge's instructions:

> You are instructed that when you deliberate on the questions posed in the special issues, you are to consider mitigating circumstances, if any, supported by the evidence presented in both phases of the trial, whether presented by the state or the defendant. A mitigating circumstance may include, but is not limited to, any aspect of the defendant's character and record or circumstances of the crime which you believe could make a death sentence inappropriate in this case. (*Texas* v. *Penry,* 1990)

The Special Issues:

Special Issue No. 1

Was the conduct of the defendant, Johnny Paul Penry, that caused the death of the deceased, Pamela Carpenter, committed deliberately and with the reasonable expectation that the death of the deceased or another would result?

Answer

We, the jury, unanimously find and determine beyond a reasonable doubt that the answer to this Special Issue is Yes.

Special Issue No. 2

Is there a probability that the defendant, Johnny Paul Penry, would commit criminal acts of violence that would constitute a continuing threat to society?

Answer

We, the jury, unanimously find and determine beyond a reasonable doubt that the answer to this Special Issue is Yes.

Special Issue No. 3

Was the conduct of the defendant, Johnny Paul Penry, in killing Pamela Carpenter, the deceased, unreasonable in response to provocation, if any, by the deceased?

Answer

We, the jury, unanimously find and determine beyond a reasonable doubt that the answer to this Special Issue is Yes. (*Texas* v. *Penry,* 1990)

Three yeses. Penry would be sentenced to die again. The prosecutors rushed into the audience where they all hugged one another. Penry stood and watched. Lieb wept, and Smith and Wright just faced each other, saying nothing. Then Penry hugged them. The defense's paraprofessionals came out and embraced Penry, too.

After reporters had collected quotes from the prosecutors and the families, a few gathered around the defense table. Wright told the reporters that Penry had asked him what the verdict was. "I think he did not understand," Wright said.

While all this was going on, six sheriffs and Texas Rangers quietly circled Penry, who, still with folded arms, looked past them at the audience. Then they took him out.

A few minutes later, when calm was restored and everyone was seated, the sheriffs and the Rangers returned with Penry—now wearing his green prison clothes.

With Johnny Paul Penry standing before him, Judge Joe Ned Dean—for the second time in his career—sentenced him to death.

CHAPTER SIXTEEN

PENRY WAITS

hat is happening to Johnny Paul Penry now is vague but scary.

After the sentence, Penry was returned to death row in the Ellis I Unit, sixteen miles northeast of Huntsville. He lives there with more than three hundred other condemned men. His home is a 5-by-9-foot cell which contains a bunk, a shelf, a sink, and a white crockery toilet with no movable seat or cover. He lives alone. He showers alone. He watches "community" television through the bars of his cell. He can be with others during a daily exercise period or during a work period in death row's clothing factory—if he is accepted, and if there is a job he can do with his limited functioning.

He can have visitors from an approved list, and he can participate in press-media interviews. Each writer, however, must make plans in advance and receive approval from the public information officer. Sadly, such meetings happen only when Penry is "going for a date"—that is, when he is scheduled for a court hearing or the death house. At other times, like the others, he has few or no visitors. Most of his relatives have faded from his life and others live too far away. The closest thing to a family will be the actors on "Days of Our Lives," "As the World Turns," and "The Young and the Restless."

Each morning at 6:00, Penry wakes up to an enormous combination of sensory overload and emotional deprivation. The television comes on. Conversations, laughter, guards' announcements, the sounds of clanging steel bounce off walls and enter his cell as a hash of cacophonic racket. There's no way to close a door and shut it out. He must live with the noise until things grow silent late at night.

The opinions of prison officials and Penry's puzzlement about what's happening count for nothing. All decisions will be made by others—in the state capitol, the Texas Court of Appeals, the Fifth Circuit Federal Court, or the U.S. Supreme Court.

But from now on, none of those courts will be interested in his guilt or innocence. Appellate courts seldom second-guess what a jury has determined. They only *review the process* by which

76

an individual was convicted. It may take months—even years—before all appeals have been played out, but if and when that day comes, things will move quickly:

An execution date will be set.

A few days before that date, Penry will be moved secretly from Ellis I Unit to the Huntsville Prison.

He will be placed in a holding cell near the death house, a small building between a cellblock and the administrative offices.

At least one guard will watch him night and day.

Officials and guards will begin work on a list of detailed tasks.

Penry may be visited by the Texas Department of Corrections chaplains, by pastors, by his attorneys, by family members, and by friends on a list of approved visitors.

The warden shall approve all visits with the exception of TDC chaplains.

No visits will be allowed after 6:00 P.M. on the day before his execution.

His last meal will be served around 6:30 or 7:00 P.M.

Prior to midnight, Penry will shower and dress in clean clothes.

The warden's office will be set up as a command post.

All participating officials and witnesses will assemble at 11:45 P.M. in a nearby lounge.

Five witnesses will be "designated" reporters (who will meet with all media immediately after the execution).

The warden may approve a few more witnesses.

All tasks from the detailed list will have been completed and checked off.

Shortly after midnight, Penry will be removed from his cell.

He will be taken to a small 15-by-30-foot chamber in the death house.

Penry will lie on his back on a hospital gurney and be strapped down.

The gurney will be wheeled next to the wall farthest from the witness area.

Medically trained individuals (never to be identified) will thread an intravenous catheter tube through a small hole in the wall and insert it into Penry's arm.

The catheter, connected to a bottle of neutral saline solution in the next room, will begin to flow.

Witnesses will enter and stand behind a rail at the far end of the room.

The warden will allow Penry to make a statement from his supine, strapped-down position.

Upon completion of the statement, the warden will say, "We are ready."

Upon hearing these words, unidentified medically trained individuals behind the wall—perhaps three of them—will introduce three additional solutions into the tubing:

> Pancuronium Bromide (to relax muscles)
> Potassium Chloride (to stop the heart)
> Sodium Thiopental (a lethal dose).

The solutions will flow into the tubing, through the hole in the wall, and into Penry's arm.

After a few minutes, a physician will step forward and pronounce Johnny Paul Penry dead.

A justice of the peace will step forward and conduct an on-the-spot inquest.

The body shall be removed from the death house, placed in an ambulance, transported to a local funeral home, and embalmed immediately.

If no one claims the body within 48 hours, it will be offered to the Texas Anatomical Board.

If the board rejects it, the remains will be buried at county expense.

CHAPTER SEVENTEEN

PENRY'S CHANCES

Even though the trial has ended, Huntsville attorney John Wright and the New York volunteers, Robert Smith, Judith Lieb, and Joseph Brennan, chose to continue their representation of Johnny Paul Penry. This means poring over more than thirty volumes of court records before preparing their brief for the Texas Court of Criminal Appeals. It will take months.

"We're in there, giving it our best," said Wright, "and we are optimistic about getting a reversal."

Those who prosecuted Penry so vigorously will do everything they can to keep Penry moving toward the death chamber. Assistant Attorney General Robert Walt, who attended the retrial, made this plain in a short, terse statement: "We need Penry."

Others close to the case say that Penry doesn't have a chance. They say appeals will be played out in about six years and Penry will be executed. Penry's case continues to be well worth watching. Consider the following facts and conditions that influence his chances:

NATIONAL STATISTICS ON THE DEATH PENALTY

Good statistics are becoming easier and easier to find. Some of the sources:

Any office of Amnesty International (AI)
The Death Penalty Information Center (DPIC), Washington, D.C.
The National Coalition to Abolish the Death Penalty (NCADP), Washington, D.C.
The NAACP Legal Defense Fund (NAACP/LDF), New York
The Southern Coalition on Jails and Prisons (SCJP), Nashville, Tenn.
The Federal Bureau of Investigation
The U. S. Department of Justice.
The American Civil Liberties Union (ACLU)

Of course, the statistics keep changing. But they are easy to understand and easy to follow. The current figures:

- Roughly 2,500 persons live on death rows across the nation today.
- We murder more than 23,000 persons in the United States each year—the highest homicide rate of any industrialized nation.
- Roughly 33,000 people now live behind bars for murders committed in the past four decades.
- In spite of the large number of homicides, only 200-plus persons are added to death row each year. That number actually is high, considering that all other Western democracies have abolished the death penalty.
- To date, 36 states, plus the U. S. government and the military, still cling to the death penalty; 14 states and the District of Columbia do not.
- How many of the 2,500 persons on death row have mental retardation? Nobody really knows. Most prosecutors, having larger budgets, tend to hire psychiatrists and psychologists who are more willing to find a person "dangerous" or a "sociopath" than mentally retarded. On the other hand, many defenses invest little or nothing in such examinations because they lack the funds.
- In 1990, we executed 23 persons.
- There were 144 executions from 1976 through 1990. (The U. S. Supreme Court reinstated the penalty in the 1976 case of *Gregg* v. *Georgia*.)

And so it goes. Roughly 23,000 murders a year—but only an average of 10 convicted murderers have been executed since 1976. That doesn't seem very many, but the implications are grim.

"IT SMACKS OF LITTLE MORE THAN A LOTTERY SYSTEM."

So spoke Supreme Court Justice William J. Brennan, Jr. But it's not a fair lottery, because everyone convicted of murder doesn't have an equal chance of being picked.

The Supreme Court intended that those who committed the worst premeditated crimes should die. Yet any prisoner who goes to the death chamber will know of hundreds who won't go—even though their crimes were more coldly calculated, more numerous, and more savage.

PIVOTAL FACTORS THAT CAN DETERMINE ONE'S FATE

Legal scholars produce large volumes when they even try to list and explain all these factors. The following list—in nonlegalistic and nontechnical terms—only scratches the surface.

The Nature of the Arrest. Was it a knee-jerk operation, or did it come after a thorough gathering of evidence?

The Status of the Suspect. Did officers perceive the suspect as valued and respected in the community or as somebody from the "fringe"?

Nature of the Confession. Did the suspect trust the police and tell all or, like Mafia kingpins, just sit down, ask for a lawyer, and shut up?

Political Clout. Does the suspect have connections?

Venue. Would Johnny Paul Penry have received a fairer trial if it had been held in Galveston, Texas, instead of Huntsville? Would his chances have been even better if the judge—by some strange legal arrangement—had ordered it to be held in Minneapolis, Minnesota?

Political Posturing. If you faced an elected judge or district attorney who had announced his candidacy while standing next to the electric chair, you might be out of luck. If the prosecuting attorney plans to run for governor, that might bear on your case as well.

Economics. Bear in mind that some states place caps from $1,000 to $5,000 on payments to court-appointed lawyers. Compare these figures with the cost of the defense for Claus von Bulow (first guilty, then not guilty to charges that he attempted to murder his millionaire wife), or Robert Chambers (the New York "preppy" murderer who, after a much-publicized trial, copped a plea and received a five-year minimum sentence), or T. Cullen Davis of Texas (see chapter 21). Justice William O. Douglas—in *Furman* v. *Georgia,* the 1972 case which suspended the death penalty—made it plain that we just don't execute a person "making more than $50,000."

Quality of Legal Counsel. Some judges appoint defense attorneys with absolutely no experience in such cases.

Juries. These "crown jewels of the American legal system," don't always sparkle as they did before both prosecution and defense eliminated prospective jurors they didn't like.

Funding. The prosecution almost always can afford more expert witnesses. The defense usually lacks sufficient money to afford the same level of expertise. A researcher comparing the two different funding streams might discover some interesting statistics.

The Pressure of Vengeance. Vengeance is something everyone senses in the courtroom but seldom speaks of. Even so, one can almost measure the degree of vengeance by the hair that rises on your forearms. It varies from case to case.

Those are only a few of the many variables that could be mentioned. Attorney Ronald J. Tabak—one who studied these variables in depth in *The Death of Fairness*—summed up the situation:

> Capital punishment remains a cruel lottery because in each stage, from the initial decision whether to seek the death penalty, through the trial, appeals, post-conviction proceedings and the clemency process, a defendant's chances of being given the death penalty depend to an astonishing degree on arbitrary and capricious circumstances rather than on the defendant's criminal and moral culpability. (Tabak, 1986)

So who usually goes to death row, and eventually dies? It is the poor with no money to pay for their defense. Almost half (49.47%) of the people on death row are minorities, compared to an almost equal number of non-minorities (50.53%)—but all are poor.

Some possess retardation and similar disabilities. We don't know yet how many have these disabilities, due to a lack of proper evaluation. Anecdotal reports on such people, however, now arrive at the statistics departments of Amnesty International, the Death Penalty Information Center, the National Coalition to Abolish the Death Penalty, and the NAACP Legal Defense Fund at an increasing rate. In a recent press statement, Michael A. Kroll, director of the Death Penalty Information Center, stated:

> What distinguishes the overwhelming majority of those on death row from other homicide defendants sentenced to life is not their records or the circumstances of their crimes, but their race (and that of their victims), abject poverty, debilitating mental impairments, minimal intelligence—and incompetent lawyers. (Kroll, 1991)

CHAPTER EIGHTEEN

HORACE DUNKINS' STRONG HEART

Amnesty International, in its 1990 Annual Report, describes the conviction of Horace Dunkins, an African American prisoner with mental retardation who died in the electric chair on July 14, 1989, in Alabama. According to the report, he was sentenced to death by an all-white, all-female jury for the murder of a white woman in 1980. According to Amnesty International, Horace Dunkins had unknowingly waived his right to a lawyer before being interrogated by police after his arrest. It claims that the jury at his trial had not been told that he had "an IQ of 65 to 69."

Despite the U. S. Supreme Court's own ruling that mental retardation was a factor juries should consider in deciding whether to impose the death penalty (see *Penry* v. *Lynaugh,* 1989), the Court refused to stay the execution.

Amnesty International described the execution:

Horace Dunkins' execution was protracted. The first jolt of electricity failed to kill him, apparently because the electric chair had been wired incorrectly. Doctors found he was unconscious but had a strong heartbeat. A second electric shock was administered nine minutes later, after the chair had been reconnected. Amnesty International wrote to the governor of Alabama, expressing its deep concern over what had happened. The governor did not reply. (Amnesty International, 1990, p. 252)

CHAPTER NINETEEN

LEON BROWN,
DEATH ROW'S YOUNGEST

fter a 1984 death sentence, Leon Brown, 16, of Red Springs, North Carolina, made the news. He was the youngest inmate on death row in the nation. Something else, however, was played down—psychological reports stating that he had "an IQ of 58." Court-appointed trial attorney Robert Jacobsen said he hadn't wanted to overemphasize his client's retardation for fear the jurors would judge him even more harshly.

Jacobsen told reporter Dee Reid: "The problem is when you start thinking about these types of crimes, that's the type of people who commit them" (Reid, 1987, p. 22).

Arguing against Jacobsen in Brown's trial was nationally known prosecutor Joe Freeman Britt, listed in the *Guinness Book of World Records* for securing more death sentences (last count: 44) than anyone else on the planet. Britt told the jury that mental retardation was no excuse: "Are you to mitigate or excuse or do away with the actions of Leon Brown because he's just like two-thirds of a million other people?" (Reid, 1987, p. 22).

The jury found that neither the defendant's age nor his retardation were mitigating factors. It determined that Brown, along with his older half-brother Henry Lee McCollum, 19, had brutally raped and murdered a young girl. According to the investigators, McCollum, with "an IQ of 74," confessed and implicated Brown. Upon receiving both confessions—the only evidence against the brothers—the investigators ceased to follow up on other hot leads. One Red Springs police officer now declares his firm belief that both Brown and McCollum are innocent.

New defense lawyers are seeking retrials.

CHAPTER TWENTY

LIMMIE ARTHER'S EASY TRAIL

L immie Arther, a 25-year-old African American—17th of the 18 children of a poverty-stricken rural Horry County sharecropper—seemed an easy pick in South Carolina's lottery for death row. On New Year's Eve of 1984, he and a 65-year-old neighbor, William "Cripple Jack" Miller, went to a store together. They cashed Miller's Social Security check and bought two half-pints of liquor, which they drank behind the store. Later Miller was found dead, a bloody ax nearby. Arther left an obvious trail. The police discovered his bloody shirt at the scene of the crime, and they found him in the upper part of his family's three-room shack, his legs hanging down through the rafters. Miller's Social Security money was in Arther's pocket.

Arther received a death sentence, but the state supreme court set it aside because of inappropriate statements made to the jury by the 15th Circuit Solicitor James O. Dunn. Dunn—who had announced his candidacy for office while standing next to the state's electric chair—removed himself from the case and his assistant took over in the second trial. Horry County Circuit Judge John H. Waller, Jr., imposed the second sentence after Arther had waived his right to a jury trial. Thus Arther stood a chance to be the third person to die in South Carolina since the U. S. Supreme Court had reinstated the death penalty in 1976.

On Friday, June 19, 1987, one month later, appellate lawyers David Bruck and John Blume asked for a life sentence or a new trial. Experts claimed that Arther possessed "an IQ of 65 and a mental age of 10-12 years." Earlier, the prosecution had never conceded that Arther was retarded. They argued that if he had stayed in school he would have learned to read and write. But Judge Waller upheld the death sentence.

Highlights:

• Jessie Miller Williams, Arther's third-grade teacher, stated that her "ultimate" goal was to teach him to write his name. She failed.

"He tried," she said. "He could remember some letters, and those—sometimes he would put some of them backwards, and some he would have forward" (Marcus, 1987).

- Attorney/Special Educator Ruth Luckasson testified that when she asked Arther to recite the alphabet, he sang the ABC nursery rhyme, got to G, then left out a few letters, and after P, the letters became garbled and out of order. Luckasson also stated that Arther didn't understand that his best chance to avoid execution was to appear as unintelligent as possible. She reported that Arther had been a model prisoner who still struggled to learn to read.

"I think he believes that the fact that he can't read is what got him the death sentence," she said (Marcus, 1987).

- Defense attorney Bruck told the judge that being poor and African American had contributed to Arther's plight.

"The mentally retarded son of a prominent person would never be sentenced to death," he said. Waller appeared offended: "That is a strong statement, Mr. Bruck."

"I don't make it lightly," Bruck responded (Monk, 1987).

- The prosecutor argued that Arther fully understood the criminality of his act or he wouldn't have hidden.

Bruck responded, "He took his bloody shirt and left it soaking at the scene of the crime. There he is, hiding in the attic with his feet sticking out. Good grief, if that's the crime of a mature criminal, I think the job of our law-enforcement agencies would be a great deal easier."

- Taken to view the dilapidated homes of both Arther and the man he murdered, Judge Waller had remarked that they would have been "better off under slavery," because then someone would be responsible for their care (Marcus, 1987).

- A later appeals court reduced the sentence to life in prison. The circuit solicitor decided not to retry the case again.

CHAPTER TWENTY-ONE

PRESSURE FROM WOUNDED NEIGHBORHOODS

Nothing can rip a hole in the social fabric of a neighborhood like a rape, a vicious attack against a child—or a murder. A murder tears apart the values that hold a community together—trust, security, fair play, orderliness, mutual helpfulness. It even rends our belief that some good can be found in everyone.

A murder creates a heart-rending situation for those who cherished the victim. It can do the same to the arrested person and his or her family—though society pays little attention to that suffering. It turns neighbor against neighbor. Those who try to understand the tragedy clash with those who would rather plunge ahead and kill the killer.

The hole that a murder rips can never be repaired. Restitution and punishment can never be enough. The victim can't come back. Bad memories won't go away. Incomprehensibles remain incomprehensible. Time, however, may lessen the pain, and people may become more wise, nurturing—or vulnerable. The local and the larger societies may even gain fresh insights into how to reduce such violent acts, and the hole may receive an awkward patch. But *nothing* can restore things to the way they were.

Even so, myriad forces—rational and irrational—go into operation in an attempt to repair the hole. People call for *justice* as a solution, even though they mean different things by that term. Litigants think justice is served when decisions are handed down in their favor. To others, it is something terrible—not something that heals but something that hurts. Some call for justice when they mean *vengeance*. Unfortunately, many who win that kind of justice will wake up the next morning to find that the raw, aching rift remains.

It has been said that Justice Oliver Wendell Holmes became angry when lawyers before the Supreme Court used the word *justice*. He accused them of shirking their job. To him, they should not seek something so vague; they should strive for the best thing that can be done in each case.

Celebrities get into the act. For example, after a gang rape and bludgeoning of a jogger in New York's Central Park, the town was torn apart. Mayor Koch, seeing it happen, made plea after plea for clear-headed thinking. Quickly, billionaire Donald Trump responded by purchasing full-page ads in the city's major newspapers:

> Mayor Koch has stated that hate and rancor should be removed from our hearts. I do not think so. I want to hate those muggers and murderers. They should be forced to suffer and when they kill, they should be executed for their crimes. . . . I want to hate these murderers and I always will. I am not looking to psychoanalyze or understand them, I am looking to punish them. (Trump, 1989)

Some politicians also hold up the death penalty as the ultimate neon-lit solution. Their announcements get large blocks of votes.

In the meantime, police departments feel the pressure. They feel guilt because they are expected to *control* crime, and they try valiantly to do just that, even though some violence that has been building for years can explode at unexpected times. One can deplore such outbursts, but predicting and controlling all of them is impossible. So the pressure remains.

Given all this unresolved pain and pressure, one can understand why law enforcement officers may unwittingly tend toward the more defenseless people. This doesn't mean they are dishonest. It's just that officers will think twice about charging a person who has money, power, and prestige. And they don't need to think twice about vulnerable people. Interestingly, inmates on death row at Ellis I, outside Huntsville, Texas, compare their situation with that of Texas millionaire T. Cullen Davis. In two separate trials, Davis was charged with the murder of his ex-wife's lover and daughter, and with an attempt to have the judge in his divorce case eliminated by a contract killer. Davis was not convicted in either case; colorful criminal lawyer Racehorse Haines defended him for a fee of $4 million (Jackson & Christian, 1980, pp. 42, 259).

Take this progression one more step: Think about what might happen when law enforcement officers who have *no substantial understanding of persons with mental retardation or similar disabilities* start looking for a suspect. Then, wonder if perhaps the arrests, and confessions, and sometimes the convictions of . . .

Limmie Arther	Morris Mason
Jerome Bowden	Henry Lee McCollum
Gayland Bradford	Johnny Paul Penry
Leon Brown	Melvin Reynolds
Horace Butler	James Terry Roach
Walter Correll	David Vasquez
Horace Dunkins	Adelbert Ward
Barry Fairchild	Earl Washington
Tommy Lee Hines	Herbert Welcome
Jerome Holloway	Johnny Lee Wilson
Edward Earl Johnson	

. . . may have been more easily obtained than the average.

CHAPTER TWENTY-TWO

A TOWN FIGHTS FOR ADELBERT WARD

Every morning after milking 23 cows, William Ward, 67, and Adelbert Ward, 59, mounted their dilapidated red tractor, chugged off their 90-acre hilltop dairy farm onto Johnson Road, and rode five miles into Munnsville, New York, for breakfast. Neither knew how to drive a car. Their brothers, Lyman, 62, and Roscoe, 70, usually stayed behind. Roscoe had a hearing impairment and Lyman—with shaking hands and an aversion for eye contact—didn't like talking to strangers, so the inseparable Bill and "Delbert" often went on without them. Sometimes, however, all four could be seen riding the tractor into town. Whether there were two or four on the tractor, facing the wind with their weatherbeaten faces and gray bushy beards (especially in the winter), they looked like Old Testament prophets hellbent on a mission for God.

Everyone in Munnsville (30 miles southeast of Syracuse, population 499) knew about the "Ward boys," whose family had lived on the same ground for more than a century. The four men lived in an unpainted, ramshackle four-room house with no indoor toilet, running water, or phone. From its dirty, cluttered interior, it was obvious that the men were outdoor people who used the house only as a shelter from storms, and for eating and sleeping. Bill and Delbert slept in the same bed.

They didn't read or write, wore the same clothes day after day, chewed and spit tobacco from sunup till sundown, and were followed by the odor of the barn wherever they went. Local folks saw them as colorful and simple and unkempt, and about a hundred years behind the times. One neighbor describes them as "little boys with old men's faces." Another estimated that, with their dilapidated machinery, they accomplished in a day what a modern farmer could in an hour. Most local folks accepted them as they were and left them alone—until June 6, 1990.

On that morning, Delbert said he got up for the milking, then tried to wake Bill. When he couldn't, he woke Roscoe, then went for neighbor John Teeple. He told Teeple something was wrong with Bill. On their way back to the Ward place, they met Roscoe, who told them that Bill was dead.

Within an hour the New York State Police began an investigation. They found nothing to indicate foul play. The brothers told police that Bill had suffered periodic headaches and weariness during the last few years. Even so, an autopsy was ordered because Bill had not seen a doctor for some time. The medical examiner reported small hemorrhages in Bill's eyelids, mouth, and windpipe. He admitted that natural causes could account for these things, but he said he couldn't rule out a murder by suffocation. He wrote on his report, "Cause of death pending further study."

That evening, the three brothers were questioned at the state police barracks in Oneida. Later, the police announced that Delbert had signed a typed question-and-answer statement, indicating that he had murdered his brother by putting his hand over his mouth and nose. They said he did it to put Bill out of his misery. They also said that Lyman had signed a document stating that Delbert had told him he planned to do it and, later, how he did it.

And so, on the day Bill Ward died, Delbert went to jail. The New York State Police and the Madison County prosecutor's office saw it as an uncomplicated, open-and-shut case. They never dreamed it would ever become more than that.

MUNNSVILLE RISES UP

Right from the start, the people of Munnsville refused to believe what the police were saying. Within the week, coffee cans with signs—HELP! DONATIONS for Adelbert Ward—appeared on the counters of every business in town. Though Delbert stayed in the Madison County jail for twenty days before his bail was set, his neighbors raised the $10,000 bail in one day. They also collected money to hire a lawyer and an investigator to study the police investigation. And not content to wait for the court, they used the media unabashedly as their pre-trial forum.

"You give me ten minutes with Delbert and I could convince him that he tore up my sidewalk, and I don't even have a sidewalk," Town Supervisor Charles Young told *New York Times* correspondent Elizabeth Kolbert. "I just don't believe he did it."

Emilie Stillwell, a waitress at The Shack Cafe, told Kolbert that everyone quickly dismissed any notion of a mercy killing: "Delbert wouldn't even know what that means." She and other residents insisted that Bill Ward died of natural causes. The police, they said, had just made a mistake and now refused to admit it (Kolbert, 1990).

Police Surprised and Embarrassed

Reporter Kolbert found the people of Munnsville reluctant to criticize law enforcement officials directly, but their efforts seemed to have embarrassed both the New York State Police and the Madison County district attorney's office. Residents also heard that the state troopers stationed nearby had been upset by all the talk about a "coerced" confession (Kolbert, 1990).

Madison County investigator Michael Donegan, defending his work on national television, showed a law official's distaste for the brothers' poverty, disorder, and strangeness—as if they must be guilty of something:

> We're talking of no running water. We're talking of a place that doesn't have indoor facilities. We're talking of two grown men who sleep in a bed together because that's the only place to sleep. They were hermits. They lived up there. They lived a very different lifestyle. And many people, I don't think approved. Or [they] were wary or afraid of that. You know, anything that's not normal or what we don't consider to be ordinary creates doubt in our mind. . . .
>
> Delbert now has been flung into sort of a sensational role within the community. I've heard him referred to as a town hero. I find that rather offensive since he has been charged with homicide. . . .

There's no doubt in my mind. I know what happened that night up on Johnson Road. And I think Delbert knows what happened up on Johnson Road. He has to live with that the rest of his life. (CBS/TV, 1991)

Neighbor Teeple countered on the same broadcast:

The differences between the lifestyle of the police and the lawyers and the detectives can't help but color how they looked at the brothers. If they're dirty, if they don't have a nice clean house, if they don't speak the language well, something must be wrong with them. Maybe they're dangerous. Ya can't really trust these hill people. . . .

It surprised everybody outside of Munnsville the way they came together in defense of Delbert. The big city man was coming after one of their boys. And they weren't gonna let him have him. Part of the sympathy for Delbert is about these college-educated police taking advantage of somebody with limited intelligence and education. That just isn't fair. (CBS/TV, 1991)

For the next nine months the police version and the town's version received repeated airings. The police called it a clean confession. Delbert, on the other hand, claimed that during the investigation, he had told the officers again and again that he didn't do it. But the investigators continued to say he did it, so finally, after more than two hours of pressuring, he thought that if he agreed with them they would let him go home.

The police said Delbert showed them how he had slid his arm under Bill's head and put a hand over his mouth. Delbert said the police showed *him* how he was supposed to have done it.

The police claimed that Lyman had signed a deposition stating that Delbert told him he had killed Bill. Lyman said he had signed it because he was upset and nervous and didn't know what he was signing. He later said that Delbert had made no such confession to him. When the police approached Roscoe, he had refused to sign anything. Later, he gave his reasons on national television:

No way. No way. No way. No way! Now if you had a cat that was half dead and you asked Delbert to put him out of his misery, he wouldn't do it. He wouldn't even shoot a cat if it was half dead. Talk about killing Bill, no way! No he didn't! (CBS/TV, 1991)

In the fall, the town held dances and raffles—all aimed at harvesting money for the trial that was sure to come in the spring. Interestingly, the brothers tended to clean up and dress a bit better. Delbert even danced for the first time in his life. All this bothered the law enforcement officials, but the town knew what it was doing. It had to get ready for the trial, too.

THE TRIAL

The trial of *The People* v. *Delbert Ward* began Tuesday, March 19, 1991, in the 81-year-old Madison County courthouse in Wampsville, New York. Most of the hundred seats were filled with Munnsville citizens—a subdued but obvious rooting section for Delbert Ward. One reporter called it the case of The People vs. Publicity.

● District Attorney Donald F. Cerio, in his opening statement, reiterated everything the police had already said about the case and, of course, claimed that Delbert had killed Bill. Defense attorney Ralph Cognetti also said the obvious—that the confession had been coerced and was based on "a phantom autopsy." Delbert, according to Cognetti, was a peaceable, impressionable, naive, compliant, submissive, simple man "with an IQ of 68."

The prosecution called a string of witnesses—neighbors and officials—who rehashed for the jury of six men and six women much of what everyone had been discussing for months.

• Humphrey Germaniuk, the assistant medical examiner for Onondaga County, reviewed his medical findings from his examination of the dead man. He presented no surprises—until defense attorney Cognetti cross-examined him.

Upon being questioned, the medical examiner replied, "Yes, I did an autopsy, but I could not label the death as a homicide. I then heard that there had been a confession, and I went back and I changed the autopsy to read *homicide*."

Cognetti asked, "If you had not heard of that confession, would you ever have been able to change your autopsy?"

Germaniuk answered, "No."

• Lyman Ward also was called as a prosecution witness, because of the statement he had signed on the day of Bill's death.

Now Lyman—on five different medications to control his anxiety attacks—stated in soft, raspy tones that he didn't know how William died and that Delbert had never told him anything about planning to kill William or about how he died.

As Cerio responded with pressing questions about why he had signed the deposition, Lyman began to shake violently and collapsed. Judge William F. O'Brien III cleared the courtroom for forty minutes while Lyman received medical attention. The judge did not require him to return to the witness stand, and changed Lyman's status from a prosecution witness to a hostile witness.

• When New York State Police investigator Robert Killough described how he and another investigator had questioned Delbert, defense attorney Cognetti criticized them for failing to take notes on the discussion or to utilize video or audio recordings. Cognetti felt the typed question-and-answer statement simply was not sufficient evidence.

• Then Delbert took the stand himself. Gripping the railing of the witness box tightly, he told the audience that his previous confession was a lie.

Questioned by prosecutor Cerio, he answered, "Why would I want to kill William? He was my best brother." Delbert seemed to handle Cerio's questions about William's death well, until they continued too long. Then he shouted angrily, "I didn't do it!"

The defendant parried questions about the night of the interrogation—"I didn't know what I was saying. I was nervous, all shook up. My brother had just passed away . . . and I'd never been in one of those places [state police barracks] before." He answered quickly and reasonably to questions about becoming the sole owner of the farm after Bill's death ("I figured that's what happens"), about wanting his own bed (he had thought about it, but it wasn't possible), about not calling the ambulance because he knew how his brother died ("No, I didn't").

Cerio noticed that Delbert often looked past him toward Joseph Spadafore, a private investigator for the defense. He accused Delbert of looking for support and asked if the investigator had told him what to say. Delbert answered, "No."

Key Witnesses

As the trial moved toward summation, both the defense and prosecution brought their best expert witnesses to the stand:

• Dr. Anthony Blumetti, a Syracuse psychologist, reported on his evaluation which included tests for intellectual capacity, academic achievement, and personality (performed Dec. 7 and 26). According to Blumetti, the defendant possessed a "verbal IQ of 69," but his "performance IQ dropped to a 60"; "the defendant is borderline educably retarded and mentally defective." He described Delbert as one who does not function well socially. He is "passive, easily threatened, emotionally vulnerable, withdrawn and anxious in social situations." Blumetti also felt that

Delbert confessed to murdering Bill in a desperate attempt to go back home. Furthermore, the defendant couldn't possibly have understood his Miranda rights when an officer read them to him.

● The next defense witness, Dr. Cyril Wecht, a lawyer and medical examiner from Pittsburgh, had studied the local medical examiner's report in detail and concluded that William Ward had died a natural death. Wecht, who had participated in the autopsy reviews of John F. Kennedy and Martin Luther King, Jr., listed the four findings that should have been present if the victim had been smothered to death: He would have been cyanotic, showing a blue tint of the skin from lack of oxygen; vomit would have been found in the throat and mouth; bruises or scrapes would have been found on the face, chin, and gums from the force of a hand; and there would have been an increased liquidity in the blood. Since the report showed none of these, Wecht had looked for other possible causes of death. He found the man's enlarged heart, liver, and spleen, and some blockage of major blood vessels in the heart and lungs; coupled with the pinpoint hemorrhages in the eyes, gums, and windpipe, these pointed toward a strong possibility of heart failure.

For more than five hours, prosecutor Cerio tried to discredit Wecht. Had he attempted to discuss his findings with the local medical examiner? No. Wecht said the autopsy report included all the details he needed to reach a conclusion. Cerio noted that Wecht had published articles in *The National Enquirer* and *Gallery*. Wecht responded that both articles related to his work on the Kennedy autopsy review panel. He added that he never read either magazine, but the articles were helpful because of their wide circulation.

● A prosecution witness, Dr. Michael Lynch, a Buffalo psychiatrist, disagreed with Dr. Blumetti's findings. He claimed that the defendant *did* understand the Miranda warnings that had been read to him: "They are very simple. A child of six or seven could understand them." Lynch said the defendant actually had "an IQ of 79 or 80." He based this on Delbert's IQ records at Stockbridge Valley school ("IQ 76.5" at age 8 and "IQ 80" at 13; Delbert left school while still in the seventh grade.) He based the IQ estimate also on his two and one-half hour interview with Delbert.

During cross-examination, defense attorney James Resti, who had teamed with Cognetti, asked Lynch if he knew whether the Stockbridge school evaluations were administered in group or individual fashion. Lynch didn't know. Resti asked if he knew what tests they were. Lynch did not know.

● Dr. Eric Mitchell, chief medical examiner for Onandaga County, took the stand to counter the testimony of Dr. Wecht. Mitchell testified that unlike the medical assistant who had performed the original autopsy on William Ward, he was certified by the American Board of Pathology, had spent ten years as a medical examiner, two years as an assistant, and had worked on "somewhere between 20 and 40 asphyxial homicides." He attacked one of Wecht's four "negative findings," asserting that William Ward might not have vomited. He held firm to murder by asphyxiation, basing his opinion on his own work with such victims, on discussions with other pathologists, and on his reading.

Closing Arguments

On Thursday, April 4, the prosecution and defense gave their summations in the small courtroom packed with more than 100 people.

● Defense attorney Cognetti spoke for an hour and 14 minutes in his final effort to convince the jury that Delbert did not smother his brother. He stated again that the defendant was a simple, honest man with a low IQ and that he would even have claimed he had killed his brother in order to get back home to the farm. Cognetti also claimed that law enforcement officials bungled this case. He questioned the training they received in conducting good investigations. He emphasized to the jury that the police took no notes and had failed to videotape or even use a simple tape recorder: "Never in my years have I seen so little paperwork coming out of so many investigators."

• Prosecutor Cerio spoke for an hour and 37 minutes, claiming that it had been proved beyond a reasonable doubt that Delbert murdered his brother William. Picking up on Cognetti's claim of honesty in the defendant, he said, "If you believe Delbert Ward is so honest . . . is he going to lie about killing his brother?"

Cerio said Ward had implicated himself when Cerio asked if he remembered that he had told them how he had held his hand over his brother's mouth: "He said, 'Yes I remember, but that's not how I did it.'. . . He told you on two occasions he committed this crime" (the two times being that slip of speech and the typed confession). Cerio covered every aspect of the prosecution's case, but he left his notes long enough to attack Joe Spadafore, investigator for the defense. Pointing at Spadafore, he accused him of coaching witnesses. Spadafore sat quietly through it all, without a blink.

JURY DELIBERATIONS

On Friday morning, April 5, Judge O'Brien gave his final instructions to the jury before a packed courtroom. He stated that to convict Ward on a charge of second-degree murder, the jurors must agree that (1) Delbert Ward had placed his hand or hands over the mouth and nose of his brother; (2) that he did so with the intent to kill; and (3) that he caused his brother's death.

At 11:30 A.M., the jury began its deliberations. More than 60 spectators stayed near the courtroom all day and late into the evening, until at 10:45 P.M., the jury notified the judge that a verdict had been reached. As the courtroom filled again, Judge O'Brien issued a stern warning to the audience: "Ladies and gentlemen, the court will tolerate no outbursts. I mean that. And if there are any outbursts, I will clear the courtroom and you can find out the verdict by reading about it in the newspapers or watching television" (Seth, 1991).

At 11:00 P.M., the jury filed into the courtroom. The verdict: *not guilty.*

The emotional level in the room rose considerably, but not a sound was uttered. Defense attorney Cognetti made his last motion—that the prisoner be released.

"Yes, Mr. Cognetti," O'Brien said. "The defendant is hereby discharged and released and is free to go, and the bail money raised in his behalf is exonerated." The spectators exploded with applause!

Delbert Ward went into the attorney's room for the red baseball cap he had worn to and from the hearings. He stopped long enough to say he wanted to thank all his friends. Then he said he had to get back to the farm to tell Lyman and Roscoe the good news.

"They'll be happy," he said. "They know I didn't do it."

THE AFTERMATH

The ending of this story seems to be still in the making. But if what happened the next day serves as any indication, one can expect many good things to happen in Munnsville, New York. Mike Dickinson, in Sunday's *Syracuse Herald American,* described the next day:

> On Saturday, Ward rose at 5:30 A.M. and went about the routine of milking cows on his farm in the hills of eastern Madison County. Shortly after 9 A.M., Ward and his brothers got on their old red tractor and rode five miles to the Country Confections Cafe. Along the way, hand-painted signs and message

boards that usually advertise church suppers congratulated them. People smiled and waved. The cafe crowd surged out with handshakes and hugs.

"I still believe in the [court] system," said Emilie Stillwell. "I'm proud to be an American."

Later the Wards greeted friends at The Shack Cafe. People stopped by the farm all afternoon.

Next Sunday, everyone plans to gather at noon on Carlon Field at the Stockbridge Town Hall for a covered-dish celebration to help raise money to pay lawyer fees.

"I've got a lot of friends," Ward said. "I want to thank them all. I don't even know who they all are."

CHAPTER TWENTY-THREE

TOMMY LEE HINES LIVES IN A LIMBO CALLED INCOMPETENCY

On May 23, 1978, in Decatur, Alabama, Tommy Lee Hines, age 25, walked around town alone. It was one of the few days in his life when somebody wasn't with him. He walked up to an office window and looked in. His face in the window and his loud, aimless talking frightened a secretary and she called police. The police arrested the loud one and took him to the station, where, according to them, he confessed to three separate rapes of white women. Hines is African American.

Without an identification lineup, the three women met Hines face to face. Two said Hines was the man who had abducted them and driven their cars (one of which had a manual transmission) to the rape scenes. The third woman was unable to identify him. But because he had "confessed" to the third rape, he was charged with all three.

Hines attended a day program at the North Central Alabama Center for the Developmentally Disabled. Repeated tests during his growing years showed that he possessed "an IQ of 35 and the mental functioning of a six-year-old." His father, Richard Hines, said, "They had Tommy driving a car. That boy can't even ride a bicycle."

Nevertheless, Hines was indicted, and immediately, an integrated group of local citizens led by Marvin Dinsmore, who was white and the father of a child with retardation, pitched in for bail and the price of a lawyer. The trial was set for October.

Almost daily during June and July, African Americans demonstrated. They occupied the city hall and the Morgan County courthouse.

Then came the Ku Klux Klan. One thousand people attended a rally on July 15 to "give support for the judicial system of Decatur and Morgan County." One month later, six thousand attended a KKK meeting, followed by a two-day camp-in on the courthouse lawn. Some carried guns. On the final day, they burned a large cross on the lawn. (All this led to a clash one year later when 53 Southern Christian Leadership Conference marchers walked into the midst of 150 Klansmen. Shots were exchanged and four persons were wounded.)

"All these extracurriculars didn't help Tommy," said Dinsmore, who had known Tommy since he was a young boy. "Most of us knew he was innocent. Why, Tommy can't even put a key in a car door, let alone drive it. But the sad thing about it all, his real situation got lost in all the hullabaloo."

The trial was transferred to Cullman, Alabama, thirty miles to the south. This change of venue failed to be an improvement, since only 130 of Cullman County's 14,200 inhabitants were African American. After a lengthy competency hearing, Hines was ruled competent to stand trial. In October 1978, he was found guilty and received a sentence of thirty years. He was sent to Kilby Prison.

A year later, the Hines family charged that their son had been homosexually raped. Officials denied it, but Governor Fob James ordered Tommy's transfer to Bryce Mental Hospital in Tuscaloosa.

On March 18, 1980, the Alabama Criminal Court of Appeals ordered a retrial. All retrial efforts were stopped on November 20, however, when the Jefferson County Circuit Court in Birmingham ruled that Hines was incompetent to stand trial.

Since then, Hines has resided first at Bryce Mental Hospital and later at Partlow State School, also in Tuscaloosa. He may spend the rest of his life in this legal limbo because he never will be competent to stand trial.

CHAPTER TWENTY-FOUR

A FRESH LOOK AT ROBERT HARRIS'S BRAIN INJURY

Robert Alton Harris, 37, had committed a crime so bad that he was scheduled to be the first person in twenty-three years to die in California's gas chamber. His date with death would have been April 3, 1990, at 3:00 A.M., but the U. S. Court of Appeals for the 9th Circuit issued a stay three days before that date.

The prosecution countered with a hurry-up appeal to the U. S. Supreme Court. They still wanted Harris dead, and on schedule. But the higher court refused 6 to 3 to lift the stay. The reason: The courts could not determine whether Harris had received proper examinations related to his brain damage caused by fetal alcohol syndrome, repeated blows to the head, and a post-traumatic stress disorder similar to that suffered by Vietnam veterans.

HARRIS'S CRIMES

On July 5, 1978, Robert Harris and his teen-age brother Daniel had decided to steal a car for a bank holdup. They spotted John Mayeski and Michael Baker, both age 16, sitting in their car at a San Diego Jack-in-the-Box drive-in, eating hamburgers. Harris pulled a gun and ordered the boys to drive to a wooded area. Daniel later told officials that when the victims tried to escape, Harris shot Mayeski twice, then ran after Baker, who prayed and begged for his life.

"God can't help you now, boy," Harris had replied, "you're going to die." Then he shot him in the head. Harris finished the murder victims' hamburgers as the brothers drove away. Later that afternoon, they held up a San Diego bank, using the stolen car.

And these murders were not Harris's first. He had spent two and one-half years in prison for the 1975 fatal beating of a neighbor. According to court records, Harris threw lighted matches on the man as he lay dying.

CRIMES AGAINST HARRIS

Harris's childhood had been incredibly brutal, too. His mother often drank herself to sleep, and his father kicked her in the stomach repeatedly when she was pregnant, in an attempt to kill the child in the womb. But Harris survived the ordeal, though he was born three months prematurely and weighed less than four pounds.

After birth, the physical and mental insults against Harris continued:

Neighbors describe daily abuse suffered by Harris as a child [the fifth of nine children]. When Harris was two, his father punched him so hard he was knocked unconscious and fell to the floor in convulsions, blood coming from his mouth, nose, and ears. It was not the last time Harris was beaten unconscious by his father. The abuse went on through the boy's early years, ending only when his mother left him on the roadside when he was 13. He was on his own from then on. (NCADP, 1990)

Two of his current lawyers, Charles Sevilla and Michael McCabe, raised the issue of Harris's brain injuries. They paid for the neuropsychological testing that led to the recent stay. They also argued that the psychiatrists appointed to aid the defense had failed to perform the psychological tests commonly accepted at the time.

"Robert Harris wasn't born evil; he wasn't a monster," said Michael Laurence, a lawyer for the American Civil Liberties Foundation who has joined in the defense. "If anyone had intervened when he was a child, I don't think he would be on death row today" (Bishop, 1990).

RECENT FINDINGS REGARDING BRAIN INJURY AND CHILD ABUSE

A recent study involving 29 murderers on death row found that almost all had suffered a serious brain injury that may have triggered the violence. According to Dr. Dorothy Otnow Lewis of New York University Medical School, their head traumas ranged from falls from trees in childhood to regular beatings.

Lewis, however, claims that brain injury alone may not always lead to violent crimes. She feels it is the combination of physical insult and childhood brutality that drives people into committing the most heinous acts: "When you have a kid who has some organic vulnerability, like a brain injury, and you add being raised in a violent household, then you create a very, very violent person" (Goleman, 1990).

In other research, in 1970 Lewis studied 95 boys at a correctional school in Connecticut. She tracked them for seven years, using records of their subsequent arrests maintained by the states and the Federal Bureau of Investigation. Those who showed no sign of brain injury or child abuse had not committed any crimes after their release. Those with brain problems *or* a history of child abuse committed an average of two violent offenses.

But those who suffered *both* brain injury and child abuse had committed an average of five violent crimes. Nine in this category had been convicted of murder (Goleman, 1990).

A separate study by Dr. Ernest T. Bryant, a neuropsychologist at the Kaiser Foundation Rehabilitation Center in Vallejo, California, supports Lewis's findings. After studying violent repeat offenders in California prisons, he believes that brain damage and family abuse can be a lethal combination. First of all, the injuries can lead to uncontrollable impulses. But the abuse in the family that they experienced or observed has provided models for acting on such explosive urges: "When such people [with brain injury] have an angry feeling, they can't step back and get objective distance" (Bishop, 1990).

POLITICAL IMPLICATIONS

Given these later developments, should California kill Harris or not? People are sharply divided on this issue. Some see Harris as a key to understanding why some people kill, and they feel it would be wrong not to follow up on this possibility.

Others say it's a waste of time. During a conversation with a reporter covering the retrial of Johnny Paul Penry (who also had suffered both brain damage and child abuse), that reporter sized up the grim side of similar trials: "I feel an unspeakable attitude in such cases. Lots of folks think it—but don't say it: 'The guy has been so clobbered and ruined by his folks, he's beyond repair. So why not just go ahead and dispose of the guy?' "

One who even refuses to consider any alternative is San Diego Police Detective Steve Baker, the father of Michael Baker, one of the murdered teenagers. By some strange twist, Baker was one of the officers who arrested Harris shortly after he robbed the bank.

"I'm not naive to death," he says, but he feels a deep pain that won't go away until Harris dies. Although Baker was divorced from Michael's mother and hadn't spent much time with his son, "Now, thanks to Harris, I never will." Years ago, Baker requested that he be appointed one of the twelve official witnesses at Harris's execution; the request was granted. He has never talked to Harris. But "before Harris dies, I want to look him in the eyes and say just one word to him: 'Goodbye' " (Bendel, 1990).

CHAPTER TWENTY-FIVE

THE DUAL-DIAGNOSED DILEMMA OF MORRIS MASON

The state of Virginia electrocuted 32-year-old Morris Mason on June 25, 1985, in spite of his dual diagnosis of mental retardation and mental illness. Mason grew up on the sparsely populated Eastern shore. Folks knew him as a school dropout, a loner, and the butt of other kids' pranks.

He spent time in three mental hospitals, where he was diagnosed as having an "IQ of 66, and schizophrenic reactions." At age 22, he lost control, committed an act of arson, and went to prison.

Two and a half years later, he left the prison, but he couldn't adjust to the outside world. Feeling himself rapidly losing control, he called his parole officer twice, asking for help. On May 12, 1978, he called again, asking that he be placed in a "halfway house" or some kind of supervised environment. The parole officer set a meeting for later that week.

That appointment was never kept because the next day Mason went on an alcoholic rampage, killing a 72-year-old woman and burning her house. On May 14, he attacked two girls, ages 12 and 13, leaving one with paraplegia.

He pleaded guilty and waived his right to a trial. Sentenced to death, he left the courtroom "talking crazy" about being "the killer for the Eastern shore" and making "the Eastern shore popular."

The Eastern shore's demand for revenge, understandably, never ceased. On the other hand, judges never stopped the legal machinery long enough to determine whether it was proper to electrocute a person so retarded and mentally ill. Virginia law requires the transfer of any prisoner diagnosed as insane to a mental-health facility. The prison warden, however, is solely responsible for initiating a sanity hearing in the case of a condemned prisoner (VA Code, 1975). As for the man's mental retardation, it was ignored.

Joseph Ingle described Mason on the last day of his life:

On June 25, 1985, Marie Deans and I visited Morris Mason in the basement of the Virginia State Penitentiary. Morris was scheduled for electrocution at 11:00 P.M. Our afternoon visit was spent talking with Morris while he packed his meager possessions in a box. He showed us letters he'd received, proud to have been sent mail even though some letters urged his killing. All Morris understood was that people were writing to him. . . .

At one point, Morris looked up and asked: "What does it mean to die?"

Marie responded: "It means you'll be with your grandmother." That seemed to satisfy Morris, and he chatted on about basketball.

Suddenly, he stopped and told Marie: "You tell Roger [another Death Row prisoner] when I get back, I'm gonna show him I can play basketball as good as he can." The concept of death eluded Morris as it does any child.

At about 8:30 the death squad came to shave him for electrocution. We had to leave. When we returned we found Morris lying on his bunk, the back of his shaved head glistening from the light outside the cell.

He turned to us and sighed: "Oh, Marie, look what they've done to me now.". . .

We sat outside the cell, the minutes slipping away. Marie held Morris's hand. He asked us about death again.

Before we could answer, his expression brightened, and he said: "Does it mean I get to order anything I want for breakfast?" For Morris, selecting his own meal after years of being fed in his cell represented the ultimate idea of heaven.

As Morris was struggling to articulate thoughts about death and dying, a shout and commotion came from the hallway. . . . I turned around to confront the warden of Mecklenburg Correctional Center, the location of Death Row over one hundred miles from Richmond and the electric chair. He was striding across the basement floor, yelling that he had to have a "private" conversation with Morris Mason. Marie and I stepped aside. . . . The warden stayed about ninety seconds, asking Morris if he had a message for the men on Death Row. Morris mumbled a few nothings, and the man left. . . .

It was 10:30, and we only had fifteen more minutes with Morris. . . . The overwhelming feeling of bidding good-bye to a child struck me. . . .

[As the death squad took Morris away] Marie and I exited through the basement door, walked up into the yard and through the administration building. Outside, the warden was holding court with the press, informing them of how "competent" Morris Mason was. Suddenly I understood why this warden had made his perfunctory visit to Morris. . . . He spoke for quite some time to the press about his ninety-second conversation with Morris. (Ingle, 1990, pp. 252-53)

After Mason's execution, Joseph Giarratano, a fellow inmate on death row, wrote a touching memoir:

When they executed Morris they didn't kill a consciously responsible individual: they executed a child in a man's body. To this day I do not believe that Morris knew right from wrong, or left from right for that matter. He just didn't want anyone to be angry with him. That includes the guards who worked the unit. The guards were always his best listeners: they had to be here for eight hours a shift anyway. And Morris would stand there and babble for as long as they would sit and listen. Back then conditions on the Row were pretty harsh, but nothing seemed to phase him. No one here, prisoner or guard, saw Morris as a threat. If he were here today he would still be chattering on about sports, and trying to please people in his own out-of-touch-with-reality way. (Ingle, 1990, p. 251)

CHAPTER TWENTY-SIX

GETTING BARRY FAIRCHILD'S CONFESSION WAS EASIEST

On September 5, 1990, Barry Lee Fairchild, 36, sat in the holding cell next to the death chamber. He was within thirty hours of a lethal injection when he received a stay. It was his sixth stay.

He was to die for the August 2, 1983, kidnapping and murder of Marjorie "Greta" Mason, an Air Force nurse in Little Rock. She was white and he was African American. Although two people committed the crime, Fairchild never implicated an accomplice. And he never confessed to actually killing her.

The trial court paid scant attention to Fairchild's retardation because a psychological examiner, using a revision of the World War I Beta examination, claimed an IQ score of 87. The Beta was a picture test used for draftees who could not read or write English.

An inmate and friend on death row had precipitated an earlier stay when he learned that Fairchild couldn't possibly have understood the Miranda rights the officers read to him. A subsequent thorough examination by two qualified experts showed that Fairchild did indeed possess "a full scale IQ of 63, a verbal IQ of 69, and a performance IQ of 61." Even so, all arguments that his confession was coerced were denied by the courts.

Interestingly, the latest stay came after Fairchild's current lawyers claimed that at least five other suspects had been cruelly beaten in unsuccessful attempts to obtain a confession to the same crime. John Wesley Hall, a local lawyer, Richard Burr of the NAACP Legal Defense Fund, and Michael Laurence, an ACLU attorney, brought the charges. They presented evidence from seven witnesses to show that members of the Pulaski County Sheriff's Department had dealt individually with all six; each one had been battered and coerced, and some were threatened with death. Two were threatened with pistols at their heads. In one instance, the officer actually pulled the trigger of his empty revolver.

Former Sheriff Tommy Robinson—later a member of the U. S. House of Representatives—was present at the interrogations, but he denied all charges of police brutality and coercion: "Mr.

Fairchild's attorneys will come up with four more liars who will claim they were beaten but have not bothered to tell anybody until now" (Marx, 1990).

Burr, Hall, and Laurence said that getting a confession from their client had proved to be the easiest: "Barry Fairchild is a very compliant person once he is broken. And he was broken."

The Arkansas Attorney General appealed to the U. S. Supreme Court to lift the stay in time for Fairchild to die on schedule. Every member of the court, however, upheld the stay.

"It's always hard for the court to stop the engine of death once it gets started," said Burr. In this case it did—for a while, anyway.

CHAPTER TWENTY-SEVEN

REGULATIONS AND RITUALS USED IN EXECUTIONS

hen we travel to any Western democracy and ask people for their opinion of the United States, the number-one issue looms clear. Most will bring up our bloody gun-knife-and-blunt-object culture, which nets 23,000-plus homicides a year. When we discuss the problem in our own country, however—in our taverns, on TV talk shows, at political rallies, or in Congress—many see capital punishment as the first and most important solution.

● Will officially killing an average of 10 people a year since 1976—especially the most vulnerable people—do any good?

● Would executing the rich and powerful help? That is, if their skilled, high-salaried lawyers would permit it.

● Will the attempts of Congress and the Supreme Court to shorten the federal appeals process help the most vulnerable people?

● If it's shortcuts to execution that we need, how short shall we make them? The Soviet press recently shed light on their secrecy-shrouded executions when a state executioner described his job. As a condemned person moves back to the cell after a final appeal has been turned down by the court, the executioner quietly walks up behind the person and, with no announcement or fanfare, gives the person a well-placed shot in the back (Amnesty International, 1991, p. 4). China does it often and quickly, with a large-caliber pistol placed in the mouth (Gray & Stanley, 1989, p. 21).

● If we choose to kill more people, how many more? Will Romania, Iraq, and Iran serve as role models? South Africa as a model has faded since President de Klerk dismantled the notorious seven-drop gallows and, so far, has refused to use the death penalty (Bruck, 1990).

● Should we try to surpass our 1933 record high of 199? Or was there wisdom in diminishing that rate until the Supreme Court abolished the death penalty in 1972?

- Do a majority of U. S. citizens now possess an evolving standard of decency that will make it impossible for them to stomach an execution rate equal to that of 1933?
- Will the recent interest in killing by lethal injection have any effect?
- "Why should society feed and clothe murderers at taxpayers' expense?" many ask. But will more executions save money? When New York considered reinstituting the death penalty, a study was done on its cost. It concluded that the average capital trial and first stage of appeals would cost the taxpayer about $1.8 million—more than twice as much as it costs to keep a person in prison for life. Added to this must be the cost of maintaining maximum security on death rows, holding clemency hearings, and carrying out the ritual of the execution itself (NYSDA, 1982).
- Will executions—or their lack—have any effect whatever on our national rate of violence? Recently, many of our leaders have been elected or appointed because they promised laws that would *increase* executions. And if they have their way they will do just that. According to current newscasts, the administration is leading the nation in this direction. In the recent get-tough-on-crime policy, it strongly endorses the limiting of federal appeals by Congress, and a much larger number of judicially ordered deaths is predicted.

On the other hand, University of California at Berkeley law professor Franklin E. Zimring says it will never happen. According to him, the death penalty is "a symbolic issue, powerful but not deep." Most people's "enthusiasm for killing increases with the distance from their actual responsibility for it" (Kamen, 1989).

THE HUMANIZING FACTOR

At the climax of his summation in the retrial of Johnny Paul Penry, defense attorney Robert S. Smith left his position in front of the jury box, walked over to Penry, placed his hands on the defendant's shoulders, and said, "This is a human being!'

Hearing Smith's statement, a man behind me whispered to his wife, "Bullshit!" No doubt about it, the jurors felt the same way—though they might not have used that term. They affirmed that Penry did indeed ride his bike to Pamela Moseley Carpenter's house and stab her with her own scissors. The local pain that resulted from that horrendous act made it impossible for the prosecution and jury to empathize with Penry's incredibly horrible childhood. Nor could they let themselves recognize the man's brain damage or retardation.

They saw him as "future dangerous"—even though many in the field of mental retardation associate daily with persons more violent than Penry. Those workers do it in structured settings, of course, and they refuse to use any form of coercion or punishment. They would never cease to see Penry as a human being, with weaknesses and strengths like the rest of us. If any of those people had testified, the jury might have learned how to recognize Penry's challenging behaviors and deal with them. Above all, they would never have demonized or dehumanized Penry as the prosecution did.

Richard Burr, of the NAACP Legal Defense Fund, emphasized this humanizing effort at a recent colloquium at New York University:

I think folks within the trial community are exquisitely sensitive to the issue of the whole danger of demonizing somebody at the same time the person's disability is revealed. What we defense attorneys are about in death cases is unfolding layer by layer of the humanity of our clients. Not to distance them from jurors and other tryers of fact along the line, but to help create an understanding. And the context in which that unfolds must not be surgical and not clinical but one of great humanity. It is one which emphasizes the varying abilities of people with mental retardation . . . the times of their heroic successes as well as their failures. (Burr, 1990)

Defense attorney Clive Stafford Smith, in an interview, addressed the same issue:

I guarantee you that if I could sit . . . any of my clients down in a room with twelve jurors and just leave them there for twenty-four hours, you would never get the death penalty in any case because they would realize that there is a human element in this guy and they wouldn't do it.

The way they do it is you have this guy in a chair, you sit him there, make him look like a criminal. You never get the human side of him. Judges and DAs say, "I'm just doing my job." That was what the members of the S.S. said after World War II. They are just doing their jobs? Bull—they are killing people. . . . It's a completely dehumanized system. If you did it in a human way, you wouldn't have any death penalty because people wouldn't be prepared to do it. (Smith, 1989, pp. 175-76)

Unfortunately, too many in the legal community do not agree. They become skilled dehumanizers of those they seek to prosecute.

THE PROCESS OF DEHUMANIZATION

Joe Ingle, long-time director of the Southern Coalition on Jails and Prisons, understands dehumanization all too well. He learned it after giving everything he had on behalf of many human beings locked into countdowns to execution:

The process of thinking here is that psychologically we have dehumanized the men on death row. Once you think people on death row are not human, you can do anything you want to them. You can give them a number. You can send them to a place to wait for their extermination and then you can exterminate them, because they are not like you and me. . . . Once you regard people as nonhuman, subhuman, less than you, you can do anything you want to them, and that's what we're doing. That's what we're doing! (Ingle, 1989)

Consider the general atmosphere . . . the uniform; having a number instead of a name; the rigid daily schedule; the isolation; the blaring television; reverberating noises on the cell block; hundreds of rules of conduct; even minor infractions placed in your record; rigid visiting hours; talking to friends and loved ones through a glass barrier or mesh screen; the shakedowns; outside the cell block, having hands cuffed behind the back, and sometimes leg irons; no window to the outside world; some lights on all night; mass punishment (if one person messes up, all must suffer); no choices at mealtime; being at the total mercy of the guards.

A major difference exists between detaining someone (as the law requires) and literally turning that person into a nonhuman. Consider these examples:

 • At the maximum security prison at Parchman, Mississippi, all the condemned wear bright red jumpsuits (Ingle, 1990, p. 105).
 • Jonathan Sorensen and James Marquart describe the relative nonstatus of death-row prisoners in Texas and how they are warehoused for death: "Death-row inhabitants are in limbo, and time spent on death row is a period of waiting. Forgotten by society, these persons are left to die a slow death before being legally executed by the state. . . . Little attention is paid to death-row prisoners, with the exception of occasional news flashes about appeals, stays, or executions. Pretending that these prisoners do not exist ignores the reality that death rows across America are holding more people now than ever before, and confining them for longer periods of time" (Sorensen & Marquart, 1989, p. 169).
 • Sorensen & Marquart also report how a death-row segregated male prisoner in Texas moves through groups of general-population prisoners on the way to visit a doctor's office. He

walks with his hands cuffed behind his back. A guard precedes, and one follows. When they come to a group of general-population prisoners, the guards get them to step aside by shouting, "Dead man comin' through" (Sorensen & Marquart, 1989, p. 174).

• The former head of corrections for the state of South Carolina recalled rotating the officers on death row. "I won't say they become attached, but they've seen the person every day and they have seen him in one role or another, maybe a repentant. By the same token if they hate the guy, you don't want them to become so callous that they say, 'It's good that son of a bitch is gonna die.' We don't want them saying things like that, so we started rotating them, especially after we knew we were going to start having executions" (Leeke, 1989, p. 113).

• Sister Helen Prejean reports that a pardon board hearing in Louisiana is a horrendous ordeal: "You sit in red chairs if you want the person to die, blue chairs if you want him to live" (Prejean, 1989, p. 100).

• In states where the firing squad is still used, the law mandates "a blank round in one of the rifles." The rationale: "None of the marksmen will know if he was the one who fired the fatal shot. Of course, anyone who has ever fired a blank and a live round cannot fail to recognize the enormous difference in the recoil of the two types of ammunition" (Gray & Stanley, 1989, p. 6).

• The head of corrections in Louisiana told Sister Helen Prejean what he aimed for during executions: "Now don't get me wrong, Sister, but it's almost like we want it to go clinically; we don't want a lot of emotion" (Prejean, 1989, p. 100).

• Texas carries out its executions as soon after midnight as possible.

• Most state departments of correction pass out press kits to interviewers and witnesses. Some of the material can be extremely helpful—statistics, laws, and bits of history. Interestingly, most of the kits contain oddity items as well. For example, the Texas kit includes a record of all the last meals prisoners requested before their death; prison photos and histories of all the women sentenced to death; and all those on death row who committed capital murder at age 17. (Texas Department of Criminal Justice, 1990)

• Many prison staff members are pulled from their regular jobs and drafted into elaborately detailed task forces when an execution nears. Joe Ingle reports on such a situation: "[In the dining hall] we were joined by a prison employee who told us about her hectic day. A secretary at the prison, she had been drafted to be a member of the Prison Information Point Squad—P.I.P.S. The acronym sounded like the nickname for a paramilitary assault team. When the deputy warden had that morning issued the stern order 'Activate P.I.P.S.' the team swung into action. 'Action' had consisted of photocopying and distributing memos, shuffling papers, and other frantic busywork" (Ingle, 1990, p. 120).

• On death rows, one often encounters guards using cold, sanitized terms to describe what they do. Advocate Scharlette Holdman attended a special hearing after the execution of John Spenkelink—the first execution in Florida after the moratorium—to investigate whether guards had beaten the man prior to his death. "The guards, prison officials, and government witnesses described the actual execution in 'guard language,' this really artificial language that they use in order to sound official and impersonal. For example, one guard testified: 'And then we escorted the prisoner to the chamber.' . . . One guard testified that he was one of the escort death squad that 'put the calipers on the prisoner' [a single handcuff with a screw handle that can be tightened down]. They put them on the prisoner so he can't kick or have any flexibility in case he wants to fight back. One prison official identified himself as 'Program Coordinator for Region Three.' Well, his program was escorting John from one cell fifteen feet away from the electric chair, into the electric chair, and putting the chest strap on" (Holdman, 1989, p. 89).

• All executioners are unidentified. They are chosen in secrecy and act in secrecy. It is strange that many people love executions, but they're not sure how they feel about the ones who do the job. In South Carolina, according to William Leeke, "The identity of the [three] individuals was known only to me and the deputy commissioner of operations. We would meet personally with them and inquire as to why they would be willing to do it, looking to see if they were emotionally stable. . . . They would go into the death house, Capital Punishment Facility, I think we called it, to make it sound more humane, but most people still call it the death house, dressed in ponchos, covering their heads, prior to everybody else's getting there, to protect their identity. They remain in the death house chamber, where the buttons that control the electric chair are located, and are brought out after everyone else leaves, again to protect their identities" (Leeke, 1989, pp. 113-14).

• Officials diffuse the tasks in an execution so that no one person needs to feel responsible for the killing. Leeke, discussing the execution buttons in South Carolina: "There are three men. There are three large buttons that all three are required to press at the same time in order to start the flow of electricity" (Leeke, 1989, p. 114).

• Leeke described his reaction: "After it's all over, you feel like you want to go wallow in mud. Because although you didn't do it personally and even though you don't want to be perceived as a total liberal or soft on crime, which everybody seems to think you are if you even say you believe there is another option, you feel like you sort of degraded yourself. . . . My concern overall is that we can become so insensitive that we can just start killing and not think a thing about it. . . . It could become so routine that we would just start exterminating people" (Leeke, 1989, pp. 115-17).

• Sometimes officials feign humanity. Advocate Marie Deans recalls such a situation: "There is a chef at the [Virginia] state penitentiary who generally wears work clothes, but when he serves the last meal in the death house, he wears a suit, a chef's hat, and pulls on white gloves! Even if he's serving french fries, because every piece of food has to be inspected in front of the execution squad" (Deans, 1989, p. 76).

• Clive Stafford Smith described a similar situation in the prison at Parchman, Mississippi. It happened prior to the execution of Edward Earl Johnson, an African American with organic brain dysfunction, who, at age 18, allegedly killed a white policeman.

"He was defended by two lawyers who had no funds, did no investigation, and basically it was an open and shut case," said Smith. The man possessed no police record—not even a parking ticket. He, with his gentle personality, became such a well-loved inmate during his eight years on death row that even some of the guards came to care for him deeply. With the Catholic Church and the American Cardinals intervening on Johnson's behalf, Smith felt sure he had won an appeal.

"But the fact was, the state of Mississippi wanted the execution," said Smith, "and the Court created absurd rules of legal esoterica to insure [it] got it."

The British Broadcasting Corporation came to Parchman to produce the documentary *Fourteen Days in May*, Johnson's last days before execution. Even the prison superintendent, Donald Cabana, tried to be human in such a dehumanizing setting. It was his job to tell Johnson it was time to move to the isolation cell, a small whitewashed room with two solid steel doors, just a few yards from the gas chamber. The room contained a tiny window above a prayer bench and a simple wooden cross.

Cabana, sensing the goodness in the man, said, "Edward, I have to tell you that I have a tremendous amount of respect for you. And you'll remember what you promised me? You'll put in a good word for me with the Man Upstairs?" Johnson nodded.

Smith, still staying close to telephones, told Johnson, "It ain't over till it's over." He still expected a stay, a commutation, or a pardon.

Then Cabana presented the strangest monologue of all: "Edward," he said, "I'm going to tell you this so you won't be surprised by anything. In a few minutes, two medical personnel will come in, and they will tape two stethoscopes to your chest. They'll also tape two EKG terminals to you. They may have to shave a little hair off to do that. They'll put them on so that they can tell when your heart stops beating. Okay? I just want you to know what they are doing" (Smith, 1989, pp. 171-86).

● Somehow, death squads possess a terrible fear that a condemned man will trick them out of an execution by committing suicide first. Advocate Deans describes one precaution: "I have to tell guys not to ask for french fries because every piece of food has to be inspected in front of the execution squad. They go through the french fries in case there is a razor blade or the like. So finally when they get their food, it's cold" (Deans, 1989, p. 76).

A RITUAL FOR AN EXECUTION

Every state utilizes a detailed ritual for ending a life. The "order of service" can be given one of a wide array of titles, but anyone reading such a document will nevertheless see it as a ritual. The following serves as an example. It appears exactly as it was printed.

1. EXECUTION GUIDELINES FOR WEEK OF ACTIVE DEATH WARRANT

EXECUTION DAY—MINUS FIVE (5)
1. Execution squad identified
2. Media & official witnesses escort identified
3. Support personnel for entrance and other check points identified
4. Medical support staff for execution identified
5. Electrician tests all execution equipment to include emergency generator and telephone
6. Superintendent briefs all CO 111 and above regarding execution activities.

EXECUTION DAY—MINUS FOUR (4)
1. Security Coordinator notified
2. Assign Death Watch Supv. & Cell Front Monitor
3. Inmate personally re-inventory all property and seal property for storage
4. Institution Chaplain notified to visit daily
5. All visiting changed to non-contact
6. Telephone check of outside line by ASO
7. Establish communications with DOC Attorney for consultation as required
8. Establish notification list and contact staff in event of significant legal change
9. Schedule meeting for crowd strategy pursuant to FSP 10P no. 65 by Security Coordinator
10. Designated electrician tests all execution equipment to include emergency generator
11. Measure inmate(s) for clothing
12. Inmate specifies in writing funeral arrangements
13. Specifies recipient of personal property in writing
14. Execution squad drill.

EXECUTION DAY—MINUS THREE (3)
No activities—Monitor.

EXECUTION DAY—MINUS TWO (2)

1. Execution squad drill.
2. Asst. Supt. Operations tests telephone
3. Electrician tests equipment to include emergency generator
4. Waiting area for execution set up by Asst. Supt. Operations
5. Electrician makes up ammonium chloride solution and soaks sponges
6. Condemned inmate orders last meal
7. Chief Medical Officer prepares certificate of death—cause "legal execution by electrocution"
8. Official witness list finalized by Central Office (12 + 4alt)
9. Executioner contacted and liaison set up for execution day
10. Asst. Supt. Programs confirms funeral arrangements with family
11. Information office arrives to handle media inquiry
12. Security Meeting held
13. External Death Watch Observer identified
14. Designated media pool observers identified by Information Office (twelve)

EXECUTION DAY

4:30 AM: The Food Service Director will personally prepare and serve the last meal. Eating utensils allowed will be a plate and spoon.

5:00 AM: The Administrative Assistant or designate will pick up executioner, proceed to the institution, enter through Sally Port and leave the executioner in the Waiting Room of the Death Chamber at 5:00 am. A security staff member will be posted in the chamber area.

6:00 AM: A. Beginning at 5:30 am, the only staff authorized on Q-1-E are:
   1. Observer designated by the Secretary
   2. Superintendent
   3. Assistant Superintendent for Operations
   4. Chief Correctional Officer IV
   5. Death Watch Supervisor
   6. Second Shift Lieutenant
   7. Chaplain
   8. Grille Gate Monitor
   9. Cell Front Monitor
   Any exception to the above designated staff must be approved by the superintendent.
   B. The Assistant Superintendent for Operations will supervise the shaving of the condemned inmate's head and right leg.
   C. Official witnesses will report to State Prison's Main Gate no later than 5:30 am, be greeted by two designated Department of Corrections escort staff, security cleared and moved to the staff dining room where they will remain until later escorted to the witness room of the execution chamber.

5:50 AM: Authorized Media Witnesses will be picked up at the media onlooker area by two designated Department of Corrections staff escorts. They will be transported to the Main Entrance of state Prison, as a group, be security cleared and then escorted to the Classification Department where they will remain until later escorted to the witness room of the execution chamber.

6:00 AM: A. The Assistant Superintendent for Operations will supervise the showering of the condemned inmate. Immediately thereafter he will be returned to his cell and given a pair of shorts, a pair of trousers, a dress shirt, and socks. The Correctional Officer Chief IV will be responsible for the delivery of clothes.

B. Switchboard operator will be instructed by Superintendent to wire all calls to Execution Chamber from Governor's Office through switchboard.

C. The Administrative Assistant, or designate, three designated electricians, a physician, and a physician's assist. will report to the execution chamber for preparation. The Administrative Assistant or designate will check the phones in the chamber. The electrician will ready the equipment and the Physician and Medical Technician or Physician's Assistant will stand by.

6:30 AM: The Administrative Assistant or designate will establish phone communication with those officials designated by the Superintendent.

6:50 AM: A. The Asst. Superintendent for Operations will supervise the application of conducting gel to the right calf and crown of the condemned inmate's head.

B. The Superintendent will read the Death Warrant to the condemned inmate.

C. Official witnesses will be secured in the witness room by two designated Dept. of Corrections staff no later than 6:50 am.

D. Authorized media witnesses will be secured in the witness room by two designated Dept. of Corrections staff no later than 6:50 am.

E. Beginning at 6:55 a.m. the only persons authorized in the witness room are:
   12 official witnesses
   4 alternate witnesses
   1 physician
   1 medical technician
   12 authorized media representatives
   4 designated Dept. of Corrections staff escorts

Any exception to the above designated persons must be approved by the Superintendent.

6:56 AM: A. Beginning at 6:56 am, the only staff authorized in the execution chamber are:
   Observer, designated by the secretary
   Superintendent
   Asst. Superintendent for Operations
   Correctional Officer Chief IV
   Administrative assistant or Supt. Designate
   Chaplain (Optional)
   Two (2) Electricians
   One (1) Executioner
   One (1) Physician
   One (1) Physician's Assistant

Any exception to the above designated staff must be approved by the Superintendent.

B. The Superintendent, Asst. Superintendent for Operations, and Correctional Officer Chief IV, will escort the condemned inmate to the execution chamber. The Adm Asst. or designate will record the time the inmate entered the chamber.

C. The Asst. Superintendent for Operations and Correctional Officer will place the condemned man in the chair.

D. The Superintendent and Asst. Superintendent for Operations will secure back and arm straps and then forearm straps.

E. When the inmate is secured, the Asst. Superintendent for Operations and Correctional Officer IV will remove the restrain apparatus and then secure lap, chest, and ankle straps. The anklet will then be laced and the electrode attached.

7:00 AM: A. The Superintendent will permit the condemned inmate to make a last statement. The Supt. will then proceed to the outside open telephone line to inquire of possible stays.

B. The electrician will place the sponges on the condemned inmate's head, secure the head set and attach electrode.

C. The Assistant Superintendent for Operations engages the circuit breaker.

D. The electrician in the booth will activate the Executioner Control Panel.

E. The Superintendent will give the signal to the Executioner to turn the switch and the automatic cycle will begin. The Adm. Asst. or designate will record the time the switch is thrown.

F. Once the cycle runs its course the electrician indicates the current is off. The Adm. Asst. or designate will record the time the current is disengaged.

G. The Assistant superintendent for Operations then disengages the manual circuit behind the chair.

H. The Superintendent invites the Doctor to conduct the examination.

I. The man is pronounced dead. The Adm. Asst. or designate records the time death is pronounced.

J. The Administrative Assistant or designate announces that the sentence has been carried out, and invites witnesses and media to exit. "THE SENTENCE OF _____ HAS BEEN CARRIED OUT. PLEASE EXIT TO THE REAR AT THIS TIME."

K. The official witnesses and media pool will then be escorted from the witness room by the designated Department of Correction's staff escorts.

7:20 AM: A. O/S Lieutenant notified by ASP to bring in ambulance to attendants.

7:30 AM: B. The inmate will be removed from the chair by ambulance attendants under the supervision of the Assistant Superintendent for Programs.

C. The ambulance will be cleared through Sally Port by escorting officer.

D. Admin. Asst. or designate will return the executioner and compensate him.

POST EXECUTION

A. The physician must sign the Death Certificate.

B. The Superintendent will return the Death Warrant to the Governor indicating execution has been carried out.

C. Superintendent will file a copy with the Circuit Court of Conviction.

D. Classification Supervisor will advise Central Office Records by teletype.

(Amnesty International, 1987, pp. 235-40)

This procedure is a far cry from Russia's surprise shot in the back or China's pistol in the mouth.

REGULATIONS AND RITUALS USED IN EXECUTIONS
VETERANS GIVE REASONS FOR THE RITUAL

The Reverend Byron Eshelman, former Supervisor of Chaplains at San Quentin:

Only the ritual of an execution makes it possible to endure. Without it, the condemned man could not give the expected measure of cooperation to the etiquette of dying. Without it, we who must preside at their deaths could not face the morning of each new execution day. (Gray and Stanley, 1989, p. 14)

Advocate Marie Deans:

There is ritual, you see, and the American people need ritual. If you deal with something straight up you don't need ritual. In the death house, ritual is the engine that drives the death machine and it encompasses the most absurd things. (Deans, 1989, p. 76)

Defense attorney Clive Stafford-Smith:

As nine-thirty approached, the "Major" in charge of death row, needing to assert his authority more loudly than necessary, said that the family had to leave. Why, reason could not really explain—but to hide behind rigid procedures depersonalizes, and somehow obscures the absurdity of something so purposeless. (Smith, 1989, p. 179)

Defense attorney Michael Millman:

All we are ever going to do is perform a "symbolic ritual," through which a minuscule percentage of society's murderers are executed. (Millman, 1989, p. 312)

On the other hand, Arthur "Cappy" Eads, Jr., Bell County, Texas, district attorney and past president of the National District Attorneys Association, believes that capital punishment separates civilized men and women from animals:

The death penalty allows society to speak to its values, to express righteous indignation for certain heinous acts. It is what distinguishes us from a hive of bees or a hill of ants. It is a way of crying out that in order to maintain a moral society, we will not tolerate that kind of conduct. (Ellis & Rice, 1988)

A FINAL THOUGHT

This book ends with more questions raised than answered. But it ends with the feeling I always have when I sit in a special spot on a grassy hill in Washington, D.C., and look down on the Vietnam Memorial. The sight of more than 58,000 names carved into black granite, the people searching for a certain name— even the thought of one U. S. President who did his darnedest to keep the memorial from being erected—makes me so awestruck I can hear my own breathing. And I hear my own breathing when I pore over the names in this book:

- The names of victims of crimes and their families, good people who suddenly—without any warning or comprehensible reason—suffered a heart-ripping assault that can never be made right, even if all the restitution in the world were made available to them.

- The names of vulnerable people who were easier to convict, imprison, and sometimes kill than others would be if accused of the same crime.

- The names of the family members of the vulnerable ones. But the order of things dictates that no attention be paid to them—forcing them to anguish alone behind closed doors.

But I also hear my own breathing when I think of a few advocates who seem to have been born before their time—certain lawyers, teachers, neighbors, friends, clergy, police officers, judges, and ordinary citizens. These people—like saints or fools—dare to walk into vortexes of unspeakable vengeance and political skin-saving, a place where someone may have been unfairly taken.

- They go because they can't stand to see vulnerable people demeaned and destroyed, simply because they don't have the prestige or power or skill or funds to make a deal.

- They go because they can't stand to see anyone destroyed because of the violence that all of us unwittingly have sown but cannot solve.

I catch my breath when they go into such a fray, for I know that, most of the time, they lose.

BIBLIOGRAPHY

AAMD (1973). *Manual on Terminology and Classification in Mental Retardation*. Washington, D.C.: American Association on Mental Retardation.

_____ (1983). *Classification in Mental Retardation*. Washington, D.C.: American Association on Mental Retardation.

Amnesty International (1987). *United States of America: The Death Penalty*. New York: Amnesty International Publications.

_____ (1989*a*). *Amnesty International 1989 Report*. New York: Amnesty International USA.

_____ (1989*b*). *When the State Kills: The Death Penalty—A Human Rights Issue*. New York: Amnesty International USA.

_____ (1990). *Amnesty International 1990 Report*. New York: Amnesty International USA.

_____ (1991). "Soviet Union: New Light Shed on Application of Death Penalty." *Amnesty Action* (January/February).

APA (1968). *Diagnostic and Statistical Manual of Mental Disorders*. 2nd ed. (DSM-II). Washington, D.C.: American Psychiatric Association.

_____ (1987). *Diagnostic and Statistical Manual of Mental Disorders*. 3rd ed., rev. (DSM-III-R). Washington, D.C.: American Psychiatric Association.

Ault, Larry (1989). "Fairchild didn't understand rights." *The Little Rock Arkansas Democrat*, March 18.

Bedau, Hugo Adam, and Michael L. Radelet (1987). "Miscarriages of Justice in Potentially Capital Cases." *Stanford Law Review* 40 (November).

Bedau, Hugo Adam (1990). Excerpts from an open letter. Washington, D.C.: National Coalition to Abolish the Death Penalty.

Bendel, Mary-Ann (1990). "Victim's father: Execution will end pain." *USA Today*, March 29.

Bishop, Katherine (1990). "The man-made disasters on death row." *The New York Times*, April 8.

Block, N. J., and Gerald Dworkin (1976). *The IQ Controversy*. New York: Pantheon.

Brown, DeNeen (1990). "Fighting for survival on death row." *The Washington Post*, July 2.

Bruck, David (1989). "Banality of Evil." *A Punishment in Search of a Crime*, ed. Ian Gray and Moira Stanley (for Amnesty International). New York: Avon Books.

_____ (1990). "Racial Discrimination and the Death Penalty." Presentation at New York University Review of Law and Social Change Colloquium. March 31.

Burr, Richard (1990). "Mental Health and the Death Penalty." Presentation at New York University Review of Law and Social Change Colloquium. March 31.

CBS/TV (1990). "Johnny Wilson: Life Sentence." *Saturday Night with Connie Chung*. May 12.

CBS/TV (1991). *Face to Face with Connie Chung*. February 11.

Commonwealth v. *Washington*, 1990. The Defense's Written Preliminary Statement. Richmond, Virginia: 4th Circuit Court of Appeals 89-4013.

BIBLIOGRAPHY

Conyers, John (1989). "A 'sexy' issue." *A Punishment in Search of a Crime*, ed. Ian Gray and Moira Stanley (for Amnesty International). New York: Avon Books.

Correll v. Thompson (1989). Memorandum of petitioner Walter Milton Correll, Jr., in support of his writ of habeas corpus, by Joseph D. Tydings and Michaux Raine III. Case No. 87-04-1787 in the Franklin County Circuit Court, Virginia. January 30.

Davis, Ron (1990). "One night of savagery triggers years of turmoil." *The* (Springfield, Mo.) *News-Leader*, September 9.

Deans, Marie (1989). "Living in Babylon." *A Punishment In Search of a Crime*, ed. Ian Gray and Moira Stanley (for Amnesty International). New York: Avon Books.

Dershowitz, Alan M. (1989). "Retarded on death row poorly represented." Syndicated Column: Judicial Affairs (United Features Syndicate). *Albuquerque* (N. Mex.) *Journal*, January 17.

Dybwad, Gunnar (1991). Personal correspondence. February 23.

Edgerton, Robert B. (1967). *The Cloak of Competence: Stigma in the Lives of the Mentally Retarded*. Berkeley: University of California Press.

_____, ed. (1984). *Lives in Process: Mildly Retarded Adults in a Large City*. Washington, D.C.: American Association on Mental Deficiency.

Ellis, James, and Ruth Luckasson (1985). "Mentally Retarded Defendants." *The George Washington Law Review*, 53 (March-May): 414-93.

Ellis, Virginia, and Dale Rice (1988*a*). "Retarded and sentenced to die." *Dallas Times Herald*, September 11.

_____ (1988*b*). "Seeking justice for retarded case: Is execution Constitutional?" *Dallas Times Herald*, September 12.

Furman v. *Georgia* (1972). United States Supreme Court, 408 U. S. 238.

Ganey, Terry (1989). *Innocent Blood: A True Story of Obsession and Serial Murder*. New York: St. Martin's Press.

_____ (1991). "Lawyer convinced of man's innocence." *St. Louis Post-Dispatch*, May 10.

Georgia State Board of Pardons and Paroles (1986). *Denial of Jerome Bowden's Application for Consideration of Commutation of Death Sentence*. Atlanta. June 23.

Goddard, Henry H. (1916). *The Kallikak Family*. New York: Macmillan.

Goleman, Daniel (1990). "When rage explodes, brain damage may be the cause." *The New York Times*, August 7.

Gould, Stephen Jay (1981). *The Mismeasure of Man*. New York: W. W. Norton & Co.

Gray, Ian, and Moira Stanley, eds. (1989). *A Punishment in Search of a Crime* (for Amnesty International). New York: Avon Books.

Green, Frank (1990). "Lawyers say confession details may have been offered by   police." *Richmond Times-Dispatch*, June 5.

Gregg v. *Georgia* (1976). United States Supreme Court. 428 U.S. 153.

Gross, Jane (1990). "California execution stayed; state is appealing." *The New York Times*, March 31.

Heilbroner, David (1990). *Rough Justice: Days and Nights of a Young D.A.* New York: Pantheon Books.

Holdman, Scharlette (1989). "Who Killed Jimmy's Mama?" *A Punishment in Search of a Crime*, ed. Ian Gray and Moira Stanley (for Amnesty International). New York: Avon Books.

Houghton-Mifflin (1985). *CorrecTex Grammar Correction System (Correct Grammar for the Macintosh)*. San Francisco: Lifetree Software, Inc.

IAPC (1980). *Training Key 353: Contacts with Individuals Who Are Mentally Retarded*. Gaithersburg, Md.: International Association of Police Chiefs.

Ingle, Joseph B. (1989). "Strange Fruit." *A Punishment in Search of a Crime*, ed. Ian Gray and Moira Stanley (for Amnesty International). New York: Avon Books.

_____ (1990). *Last Rights: 13 Fatal Encounters with the State's Justice*. Nashville: Abingdon Press.

InterServ (1986). *Report of the First Inter-State Seminar on Self-Advocacy*. Princeton, N. J., March 21-22. New York: InterServ, Suite 410, United Nations Plaza.

_____ (1987). *Report of the Second Inter-State Seminar on Self-Advocacy*. Stamford, Conn., December 4-5. New York: InterServ, Suite 410, United Nations Plaza.

Jackson, Bruce, and Diane Christian (1980). *Death Row: A Devastating Report on Life Inside the Texas Death House*. Boston: Beacon Press.

Johnson, Robert (1990). *Death Work: A Study of the Modern Execution Process*. Pacific Grove, Calif.: Brooks/Cole Publishing Co.

Kamen, Al (1989). "Number of executions drops despite forecast." *The Washington Post*, November 6.

Kernan, Keith, and Susan Sabsay (1984). "Getting there: Directions Given by Mildly Retarded and Nonretarded Adults." *Lives in Process: Mildly Retarded Adults in a Large City*, ed. Robert Edgerton. Washington, D.C.: American Association on Mental Deficiency.

Kolberg, Elizabeth (1990). "A dairy town doubts brother killed brother." *New York Times*, July 17.

Kroll, Michael A. (1991). Press Kit. Washington, D.C.: National Death Penalty Information Center (January).

Launderville, Dena (1991). Personal correspondence (with a voted permission by Project II to publish their letter to Governor Ashcroft).

Leeke, William D. (1989). "Behind Closed Doors." *A Punishment in Search of a Crime*, ed. Ian Gray & Moira Stanley (for Amnesty International). New York: Avon Books.

Luckasson, Ruth (1990). "Mental Health and the Death Penalty." Presentation at New York University Review of Law and Social Change Colloquium. March 31.

Marcus, Ruth (1987). "Retarded killer's sentence fuels death-penalty debate." *The Washington Post,* June 23.

———— (1990). "On death row, how many appeals are enough?" *The Washington Post,* June 9.

Marx, Claude R. (1990). "Groups argue for respite." *Arkansas Democrat,* September 5.

Maurer, Bill (1990*a*). *The Marionville* (Mo.) *New Press,* September 10.

———— (1990*b*). "Eyewitness supports Johnny Wilson's alibi." *The Marionville* (Mo.) *New Press,* December 3.

Menninger, Karl (1966). *The Crime of Punishment.* New York: Viking Press.

Millman, Michael (1989). "California Dreaming." *A Punishment in Search of a Crime*, ed. Ian Gray and Moira Stanley (for Amnesty International). New York: Avon Books.

Monk, John (1987). "Judge upholds death sentence for retarded S. C. ax murderer." *The Charlotte Observer,* June 20.

Montgomery, Bill (1986). "Bowden's execution stirs protest." *The Atlanta Journal,* October 13.

NAACP/LDF (1991). *Death Row U.S.A. Newsletter.* New York: NAACP Legal Defense Fund. January 21.

NCADP (1990). *Execution Alert Newsletter.* Washington, D.C.: National Coalition to Abolish the Death Penalty. February.

Norley, Dolores (1972*a*). "Police Education: How to Recognize and Handle Persons with Retardation." Presentation at Fifth International Congress on Mental Retardation, The International League of Societies for Persons with Mental Handicaps. Montreal. October 2.

———— (1972*b*). "Due process is overdue: Who is protecting whom from what?" Keynote Address at Seminar on Retarded Citizens and the Law Enforcement Process. St. Louis, Mo. October 29.

———— (1974). "Restoration or Revenge?" Keynote Address at Symposium on Persons with Retardation and Corrections. University of Oregon. Eugene. February 17.

———— (1984). "Being Retarded Is the First Offense: Perplexities with Police and Courts." Keynote Address at Texas Department of Mental Health and Mental Retardation Symposium. Houston. May 2.

———— (1985). "Defendants with Retardation: Artless People Caught in an Unaccustomed Maze." Keynote Address at Individual Justice Plan Symposium. Omaha, Neb. April 29.

———— (1986). "Defendants with Retardation: Quintessential Cast-offs." Keynote Address at Developmentally Disabled Offender Program. Sioux Falls, S. Dak. June 4.

———— (1990). Personal Correspondence. August 25.

NYSDA (1982). *Capital Losses: The Price of the Death Penalty in New York State.* A report from the New York State Defense Association to the Senate Finance Committee and Other Sections of the State Legislature. April.

Penry v. *Lynaugh Amicus* (1988). No. 87-6177, United States Supreme Court, October 1988 term. Amicus Members: American Association on Mental Retardation; American Psychological Association; Association for Retarded Citizens of the United States; The Association for Persons with Severe Handicaps; American Association of University Affiliated Programs for the Developmentally Disabled; American Orthopsychiatric Association; New York State Association for Retarded Children, Inc.; National Association of Private Residential Resources; National Association of Superintendents of Public Residential Facilities for the Mentally Retarded; Mental Health Law Project; National Association of Protection and Advocacy Systems.

Penry v. *Lynaugh* (1989). The United States Supreme Court 109 S.C. 2934.

Perske, Robert (1978). Report to the President. *Mental Retardation: The Leading Edge—Service Programs That Work.* Washington, D.C.: President's Committee on Mental Retardation.

———— (1990). *Texas* v. *Penry,* personal courtroom notes. Huntsville. May 10-16; July 2-17.

Powers, Linda (1990). "We All Want Johnny Home." Copyright 1990 by Linda Powers.

Prejean, Sister Helen (1989). "A Pilgrim's Progress." *A Punishment in Search of a Crime*, ed. Ian Gray and Moira Stanley (for Amnesty International). New York: Avon Books.

Priest, Dana (1989). "At each step, justice faltered for Virginia man." *The Washington Post,* July 16.

Radelet, Michael L., ed. (1989). *Facing the Death Penalty: Essays on a Cruel and Unusual Punishment.* Philadelphia: Temple University Press.

Reid, Dee (1987). "Unknowing Punishment." *Student Lawyer* (May).

Rosenbaum, Ron (1990). "Travels with Dr. Death." *Vanity Fair* (May).

RTC/IL (1987). *Guidelines for Reporting and Writing About People with Disabilities.* Lawrence, Kan.: Research and Training Center on Independent Living, University of Kansas.

Rubin, Ellis (1989). "Changing justice." *USA Today,* November 27.

Seth, Dale (1991). "Ward innocent." *Oneida* (N.Y.) *Dispatch,* April 6.

Smith, Clive Stafford (1989). "An Englishman Abroad." *A Punishment in Search of a Crime*, ed. Ian Gray and Moira Stanley (for Amnesty International). New York: Avon Books.

BIBLIOGRAPHY

_____ (1990). "Issues Involving Persons with Mental Retardation in the Criminal Justice System." Address at American Association on Mental Retardation. Atlanta, Ga. May 29.

Smith, Patricia M. (1986). Application of Jerome Bowden for a 90-Day Stay of Execution and for Commutation of His Sentence of Death. Before the Board of Pardons and Paroles, State of Georgia.

Sorensen, Jonathan R., and James W. Marquart (1989). "Working the Dead." *Facing the Death Penalty: Essays on a Cruel and Unusual Punishment,* ed. Michael L. Radelet. Philadelphia: Temple University Press.

Styron, William (1989). "The Virginian." *A Punishment in Search of a Crime,* ed. Ian Gray and Moira Stanley (for Amnesty International). New York: Avon Books.

Tabak, Ronald J. (1986). "The Death of Fairness: The Arbitrary and Capricious Imposition of the Death Penalty in the 1980s". *New York University Review of Law and Social Change.* 14/4: 798-848.

Taubman, Bryan (1988). *The Preppy Murder Trial.* New York: St. Martin's Press.

Taylor, John (1989). "Downhill Racer." *A Punishment in Search of a Crime,* ed. Ian Gray and Moira Stanley (for Amnesty International). New York: Avon Books.

Texas Department of Criminal Justice (1990). *Execution Information.* Huntsville: The Public Information Office.

Texas v. Penry (1980). No. 6572. Groveton, Texas: District Court of Trinity County, 258th Judicial District. March 11-12.

Texas v. Penry (1990). No. 15, 977C. Huntsville, Texas: District Court of Walker County. 278th Judicial District. Charge of the Court. July 17.

Thompson, Tracy (1987). "Executions of retarded opposed." *The Atlanta Journal,* January 6.

Thurston, Scott (1988). "Death penalty ban urged for the retarded." *The Atlanta Constitution,* February 16.

Tidyman, Ernest (1974). *Dummy.* Boston: Little, Brown & Co.

Totenberg, Nina (1988). "Capital Punishment and the Mentally Retarded." *All Things Considered.* National Public Radio. December 27.

Trump, Donald (1989). Selected statements from newspaper advertisements. Phil Hamill, "T Without Sympathy." *Esquire.* (December).

VA Code (1975). Virginia Code 19.2.177.

WCBS (1991). The Morning News, 10:21 A.M. New York: WCBS Radio.

Webb, Ollie (1991). Project II letter to Governor John Ashcroft. Omaha, Neb. March 7.

Whitley, Chris (1989). *The* (Springfield, Mo.) *News-Leader,* June 25.

Wicker, Tom (1975). *A Time to Die.* New York: *New York Times* Books.

Wilson v. State of Missouri (1990). Appeal to the Missouri Court of Appeals Requesting an Oral Argument (Southern District). Case No. 16559-2.

Wilson v. State of Missouri (1991a). Appellant's Reply Brief, Supreme Court of Missouri, Case No. 73285.

Wilson v. State of Missouri (1991b). Motion to Supplement the Record on and/or in the Alternative to Remand to the Circuit Court for a Hearing on Newly Discovered Evidence. Supreme Court of Missouri. Case No. 73285.

Zehr, Howard (1991). "Who Will Defend Herbert Welcome?" *The Newsletter.* Akron, Penn.: Office of Criminal Justice, Mennonite Central Committee.

INDEX